A GUIDE TO LEARNING

HIRAGANA

AND

KATAKANA

A GUIDE TO LEARNING
HIRAGANA
AND
KATAKANA

Kenneth G. Henshall with Tetsuo Takagaki

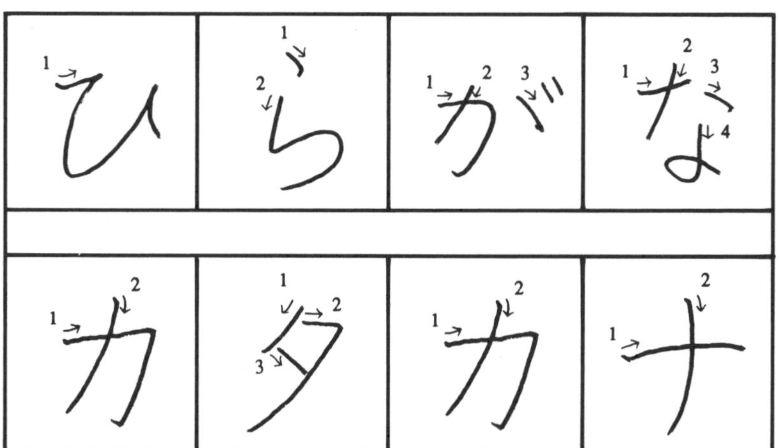

TUTTLE PUBLISHING
Boston • Rutland, Vermont • Tokyo

Published by Tuttle Publishing,
An imprint of Periplus Editions (HK) Ltd.

LCC Card No. 90-70374
ISBN 0-8048-1663-8

First edition, 1990
Tenth printing, 2002

Printed in Singapore

Distributed by:

Japan & Korea
Tuttle Publishing
RK Building 2nd Floor
2-13-10 Shimo-Meguro, Meguro-ku
Tokyo 153 0064
Tel: (03) 5437 0171
Fax: (03) 5437 0755

North America
Tuttle Publishing
Airport Industrial Park
364 Innovation Drive
North Clarendon, VT 05759-9436
Tel: (802) 773 8930
Fax: (802) 773 6993

Asia Pacific
Berkeley Books Pte. Ltd.
130 Joo Seng Road #06-01/03
Singapore 368357
Tel: (65) 280 1330
Fax: (65) 280 6290

CONTENTS

HOW TO USE THIS BOOK

The main aim of this book is to help students achieve competence in reading and writing *kana,* the phonetic symbols that are fundamental to written Japanese. The book starts with a section entitled An Explanation of *Kana,* which contains everything the student will need to know about the two *kana* systems of *hiragana* and *katakana*. Part I of the workbook section then systematically introduces each *hiragana* symbol, voiced form, and combination, and provides ample practice and review. Part II does the same for *katakana,* while Part III provides an overall review.

The Explanation of *Kana* outlines the function and origin of *kana,* the difference between the two *kana* systems, the various sounds, the combinations, and the conventions of usage. It attempts to be detailed and thorough so that it can be used for reference at any stage. Though all the information about *kana* is grouped together in this one section for ease of reference, it is not expected that the student will read it all before starting on the practice pages. In fact, to do so might give the impression that *kana* are perhaps rather formidable, which is not really the case at all. (Just ask any Japanese child!) We recommend that the student start work on the *hiragana* practice pages after reading the first three subsections — on the function, origin, and basic sounds of *kana*. After finishing practice of the forty-six basic *hiragana* symbols the student should go back to the Explanation and read the subsection on additional sounds, then work through the rest of the *hiragana* practice pages before moving on to the *katakana* practice. The final subsection, on other points to note, is mostly concerned with special *katakana* combinations and can be left until the appropriate point in the *katakana* practice pages, just prior to the final review. Students may modify this order, but we recommend finishing practice of one *kana* system before moving on to the next.

In the practice pages of Parts I and II each *kana* symbol is allotted half a page, permitting plenty of writing practice in the boxes given. We suggest working in pencil, rather than ink, as this will allow for erasing and repeated use. Stroke order and a pronunciation guide are also given for each symbol. In addition, for each symbol there is an illustration of its graphic evolution from its "parent" character (see Explanation of *Kana*) and a reference number for that character as it occurs in *A Guide to Remembering Japanese Characters* (Charles E. Tuttle Company, 1988), together with the character's pronunciation. This may be of interest to readers wishing to continue their studies of written Japanese to an advanced level. (However, some of the original characters are no longer commonly used and therefore are not included in *A Guide to Remembering Japanese Characters*.)

After approximately every ten symbols there are "mini review" pages for further practice, this time using whole words. These are cumulative, containing symbols not only from the group just completed but from earlier groups. The mini reviews can be used purely for copying practice, or, by covering the cue *kana* on the left side of the page, as more challenging writing exercises. They can also be used as vocabulary exercises.

Part III, the Final Review, contains exercises, quizzes, and "do-it-yourself" charts. Unlike the reviews in the first two parts it combines the two *kana* systems, as is natural in Japanese texts. And for a more natural effect the boxes used earlier in the book to help achieve even spacing and proper stroke lengths are dispensed with in this final part.

The words appearing in the reviews have been carefully chosen in keeping with an additional aim of this book, which is to expose readers to key words related to Japanese society and culture. The prime criterion for selecting review words was their suitability for practicing the *kana* symbols, but we thought it would be helpful to students if in addition these words could, whenever possible, have particular relevance to Japanese culture. About half of the 450 or so vocabulary items in the book fall into this category. It is beyond the scope of the book to explain these in detail, but students who take the trouble to find out more about them will be rewarded with a broadened appreciation of Japan's society and culture. In short, we intend that these words should be used as a sort of checklist for an exploration of Japan, rather than simply memorized as isolated vocabulary items.

Readers will occasionally encounter a semicolon between English equivalents given for a Japanese review word. This indicates that the Japanese word is a homophone, that is, a word having a different meaning but the same sound as another. Normally these homophones would be written with different characters, but when expressed in phonetic *kana* script or romanization such differentiation is not possible. The English words separated by a semicolon thus refer to different Japanese words sharing the same *kana* form. (Commas between English words simply indicate nuances of the same word.) It should also be noted that there is sometimes a subtle difference in intonation between "homophones," which cannot be determined from the *kana* or romanization.

Finally, readers are advised to seek specialist or native-speaker guidance on intonation and pronunciation. It should be appreciated that the pronunciation guides given in this book can only ever be approximate, owing to the variety in pronunciation of the same English word in different parts of the world. Also, some Japanese sounds cannot be precisely represented by English letters. The Japanese "r," for example, actually falls between the English "r" and "d." But remember that, with both speaking and writing, practice makes perfect!

AN EXPLANATION OF *KANA*

The Function of *Kana*

Kana are purely phonetic symbols. That is, they are written representations of pronunciation. They can express the entire Japanese language in writing, though in practice the written language uses a mixture of *kana* and *kanji* (characters taken from Chinese).

There are two *kana* systems: *katakana* and *hiragana*. *Katakana* is now mainly used for words taken from languages other than Chinese. *Hiragana* is the more important of the two systems, and is used for everything not written in *katakana* or *kanji*. *Kanji* show meanings of words, though they also have pronunciations. Normally they are used for nouns and the the unchanging part (the stem) of verbs, adjectives, and adverbs, while *hiragana* symbols are used for the changing parts (notably endings). For example, the verb *iku* means "go," while *ikanai* means "not go." The stem is *i-*, and this is usually written with a *kanji*, while the variable endings *-ku* and *-kanai* are written in *hiragana*. *Hiragana* is also used to write particles, and other words where *kanji* are not appropriate. To all intents and purposes the two *kana* systems are not interchangeable, and are rarely mixed within a given word. The rule is: ***katakana* for non-Chinese loan words, *hiragana* and *kanji* for the rest.**

The student of Japanese should ideally aim to learn all the two thousand *kanji* in common use. They play a very practical role in graphically and distinctively conveying the meaning of a written statement, unlike a purely phonetic script, and thereby aid rapid understanding. And naturally, no one can expect to read unedited Japanese texts without a knowledge of *kanji*. However, learning the *kanji* is a time-consuming task. Many of them are structurally complex, and many have a wide range of meanings and pronunciations.

Kana, on the other hand, are much fewer in number, with only forty-six basic symbols in each of the two systems. They are simple to write, and, with very few exceptions, they have fixed pronunciations. If you don't know the *kanji* for a particular word, but know the pronunciation, you can just express that entire word in *kana* (*hiragana*, that is; remember that *katakana* is for non-Chinese foreign words). In other words, while not ideal, ***kana* (*hiragana*) can substitute for *kanji*.** This means that even beginners can express themselves in functional written Japanese with relatively little effort.

The Origin of *Kana*

The word *kana* derives from *karina,* meaning "borrowed name," for the *kana* symbols are simplified forms of certain borrowed Chinese characters used for their sound (though, confusingly, the same characters lent their meaning in other contexts). The prefix *hira-* means "ordinary," with connotations of "informal" and "easy," and in this particular case "cursive." Thus *hiragana* means "ordinary (cursive) *kana,*" and indeed *hiragana* has traditionally been the more commonly used of the two systems, and the more cursive. The *hiragana* symbols are simplifications of whole Chinese characters. For example, the *kana* あ (pronounced like the "a" in "car") derives from a cursive rendition of the character 安 (pronounced "an"). *Kata-* means "one side" or "partial," pointing to the fact that *katakana* symbols derive from one part of a Chinese character. For example, イ (pronounced like "ee" in "meet") is the left-hand part of the character 伊 (also pronounced "ee").

Both systems evolved around the end of the eighth century. In those early days *hiragana* was used mostly by women, while men preferred to use the more angular *katakana*. However, these associations have long since disappeared.

The Basic Sounds Represented by *Kana*

Kana symbols basically represent syllables, and the *kana* systems are therefore syllabaries rather than alphabets. Generally the syllables are crisp and clear combinations of one consonant and one following vowel, or one vowel by itself. There is only one consonant that exists as a syllable and *kana* symbol in its own right, *n*.

The use of English letters to refer to Japanese sounds and symbols can produce a number of apparent irregularities. Among other things a combination of consonant and vowel in Japanese will not necessarily have the same pronunciation as in English. For example, while ふ is found in the *h* group (see the table that follows), its pronunciation is actually closer to the English sound "fu" than "hu." To facilitate pronunciation the romanization used in this book is a version of the Hepburn system, which transcribes ふ as *fu* rather than *hu,* but readers should appreciate that there is no direct equivalent in Japanese to an English "f." Similar cases of convenient but seemingly irregular romanization are found in the *s* group and *t* group. This may begin to seem complicated, but in fact correspondence in Japanese between *kana* spelling and pronunciation is much simpler than in the case of English and its alphabet. Attempts to express certain loan words in *katakana* can seem awkward, but that is really a problem relating to the Japanization of non-Japanese words, rather than to the *kana* system itself.

Each of the two *kana* systems contains the same basic forty-six syllables, arranged in the same order. The basic syllabaries are as follows (combined for convenience, with the *katakana* written slightly smaller).

VOWELS

CONSONANTS

	a	i	u	e	o
	あ ア a	い イ i	う ウ u	え エ e	お オ o
k	か カ ka	き キ ki	く ク ku	け ケ ke	こ コ ko
s	さ サ sa	し シ shi	す ス su	せ セ se	そ ソ so
t	た タ ta	ち チ chi	つ ツ tsu	て テ te	と ト to
n	な ナ na	に ニ ni	ぬ ヌ nu	ね ネ ne	の ノ no
h	は ハ ha	ひ ヒ hi	ふ フ fu	へ ヘ he	ほ ホ ho
m	ま マ ma	み ミ mi	む ム mu	め メ me	も モ mo
y	や ヤ ya		ゆ ユ yu		よ ヨ yo
r	ら ラ ra	り リ ri	る ル ru	れ レ re	ろ ロ ro
w	わ ワ wa				を ヲ wo
ん ン n — n					

This order is known as the *gojūonjun,* meaning "the fifty sounds order." In fact, there are now only forty-six basic symbols (sounds) officially in use. *Yi, ye,* and *wu* do not exist. *Wi* (ゐ/ヰ) and *we* (ゑ/ヱ) were officially removed from the list in 1946 since the sounds were considered sufficiently close to *i* and *e* to be represented by the symbols for these. However, the symbols for *wi* and *we* are still encountered on rare occasions.

The *gojūonjun* is the standard order followed by dictionaries and other reference works. It is therefore particularly important to remember it. To this end, the following mnemonic, which is a modified version of one taught by Professors Dunn and O'Neill of the University of London, may be helpful.

Ah, kana signs! Take note how many you read well (n).

The reader will have taken note of the fact that the first letters of these words follow the *gojūonjun* consonant headings. With apologies to mathematicians, even the syllable *n* (ん) is represented, by the mathematical symbol "n" indicating the utmost number (in this case 92, the sum of the two *kana* systems).

The syllable *n* (ん) is sometimes called the "independent n" but in fact it can never be used truly independently. Nor can it ever start a word. When working from romanization it is sometimes difficult to tell whether a non-initial *n* followed by a vowel is a syllable from the *n*- group, or whether it is *n* (ん) followed by an independent vowel. For example, *tani* could be either たに(valley) or たんい(unit). Context usually makes this clear. To avoid ambiguity some romanization systems use an apostrophe after the *n* that represents ん. Thus たんいcan be romanized as *tan'i*. Note also that in romanization ん is sometimes written as *m* before a *p, b,* or *m,* as in *shimbun* for *shinbun* (newspaper). This practice is by no means universally followed (and is not followed in this book), but its existence does indicate one of the exceptional cases where the pronunciation of a *kana* symbol could be said to vary slightly according to context.

Additional Sounds Represented by *Kana*

In addition to the forty-six basic symbols, there are sixty-one classified modifications and combinations in each system, and a few further special combinations as well. This may sound alarming, but in fact it involves only a handful of new points to learn.

The first is the *dakuon,* meaning "voiced sound" or "hardened sound." Sounds starting with the unvoiced consonants *k, s, t,* and *h* are voiced as *g, z/j, d/z/j,* and *b* respectively if the diacritical marks ﾞ are added to the upper right side of the basic *kana* symbol, as shown in the following table. (See also pp. 52~56.) The table also shows *handakuon,* meaning "half-voiced sound," which applies only to sounds starting with *h*. The addition of a small circle ° to the upper right side of the appropriate basic *kana* symbol changes the pronunciation from *h* to *p* (as opposed to changing it to *b* in the case of the full *dakuon*).

	VOWELS				
CONSONANTS	a	i	u	e	o
g	が ガ ga	ぎ ギ gi	ぐ グ gu	げ ゲ ge	ご ゴ go
z/j	ざ ザ za	じ ジ ji	ず ズ zu	ぜ ゼ ze	ぞ ゾ zo
d/z/j	だ ダ da	ぢ ヂ ji	づ ヅ zu	で デ de	ど ド do
b	ば バ ba	び ビ bi	ぶ ブ bu	べ ベ be	ぼ ボ bo
p	ぱ パ pa	ぴ ピ pi	ぷ プ pu	ぺ ペ pe	ぽ ポ po

Ji and *zu* are written じ and ず, except when they clearly derive from *chi* (ち) and *tsu* (つ) in compounds or repeated symbols. For example, *hanaji* (nosebleed, from *hana* [nose] and *chi* [blood]) is はなぢ, and *tsuzuku* (continue, from *tsutsuku*) is つづく.

A combination of a consonant and *y-* is known as a *yōon,* meaning "contracted sound." Any of the seven basic consonants *k, s, t, n, h, m,* or *r,* or voiced or half-voiced consonants, can be used. The symbol that represents these consonants plus *i,* for example き *(ki)* or し *(shi),* is followed by a symbol from the *y-* group — either *ya, yu,* or *yo* as appropriate. This second symbol is written smaller, while the *i* sound is barely pronounced and is dropped in romanization. Thus *kyo* is expressed as きょ and *shu* (*syu* in some romanization systems) as しゅ . If the よ or ゆ of our examples were written the same size as the preceding symbols, then they would be treated as uncombined symbols and read *kiyo* or *shiyu* respectively. Full tables are given below. (See also pp. 59~62.)

	a	u	o
ky	きゃ キャ kya	きゅ キュ kyu	きょ キョ kyo
sh	しゃ シャ sha	しゅ シュ shu	しょ ショ sho
ch	ちゃ チャ cha	ちゅ チュ chu	ちょ チョ cho
ny	にゃ ニャ nya	にゅ ニュ nyu	にょ ニョ nyo
hy	ひゃ ヒャ hya	ひゅ ヒュ hyu	ひょ ヒョ hyo
my	みゃ ミャ mya	みゅ ミュ myu	みょ ミョ myo
ry	りゃ リャ rya	りゅ リュ ryu	りょ リョ ryo

	a	u	o
gy	ぎゃ ギャ gya	ぎゅ ギュ gyu	ぎょ ギョ gyo
j	じゃ ジャ ja	じゅ ジュ ju	じょ ジョ jo
j	ぢゃ ヂャ ja	ぢゅ ヂュ ju	ぢょ ヂョ jo

by	びゃ ビャ bya	びゅ ビュ byu	びょ ビョ byo
py	ぴゃ ピャ pya	ぴゅ ピュ pyu	ぴょ ピョ pyo

Note that ヂ combinations rarely occur.

Some consonants — essentially *k, s, t,* and *p* — can be doubled by inserting a small *tsu* (っ or ッ) in front of them. This combination is known as a *sokuon* (double consonant). Thus *gakki* (school term) is expressed as がっき. The little っ or ッ is not pronounced as such, but the consonant that follows it is given, as it were, a double amount of time for its pronunciation. It is important to apply this extra time to the consonant only, and not to the following vowel. Thus the word in our example should be pronounced *gakki* and not *gakkii*. These double consonants can never begin a word. (See also pp. 57~58.)

Students commonly make the mistake of trying to write a double *n,* as in words like *annai* (guide), with a small っ. The correct way is to use ん to represent the first *n*. Thus *annai* should be written あんない.

The lengthening of vowels (including the vowel sound of syllables in which a consonant precedes the vowel) can also cause errors, especially in the case of the long *o*. In romanization long vowels are usually indicated (if at all) either by writing the vowel twice or by a macron, as in *uu* or *ū* for a long *u*. For loan words in *katakana,* a barlike symbol ー (or | with vertical script) is used. Thus *rabā* (rubber) is written ラバー. In *hiragana,* the vowels *a, i, u,* and *e* are doubled by simply writing あ, い, う, or え respectively after the preceding symbol. Thus *okāsan* (mother) is written おかあさん. (The doubling of *a* and *e* actually occurs infrequently in *hiragana.* What sounds like a long *e* is usually *e* followed by *i,* as in せんせい, *sensei* [teacher].) A long *o* can sometimes be formed by doubling in the same way as with other vowels, that is, by adding お, but it is more commonly formed by adding う *(u).* Thus *sō* (so, thus) is written そう. The long *o* that takes お was once pronounced slightly differently from the long *o* that takes う, but that is no longer true, and it is necessary to learn each word with a long *o* sound case by case. Fortunately, there are only a few common words that require the addition of お as opposed to う. These include *ōkii* (big, おおきい), *ōi* (many, おおい), *tōi* (far, とおい), *tō* (ten, とお), and *tōri* (way, road, とおり). Students should take particular care not to be misled by the common romanization practice of writing a long *o* as *oo,* when in *hiragana* it is usually お *(o)* plus う *(u).*

Caution is also needed when transcribing from *kana* to romanization. Always check that an apparent long vowel really is a long vowel, and not two unlinked vowels. A typical case of the latter is a verb whose variable ending starts with the same vowel as the last vowel of the stem, or appears to combine with it to make a long *o*. For example, the verb そう, meaning "go with," should always be romanized as *sou* and not *sō* or *soo*. (By contrast, そう meaning "thus," being a genuine long vowel, is romanized as *sō* or *soo*.) Similarly, *suu* is the romanization for the verb すう (suck), rather than *sū,* and *kiite* is the way to romanize the suspensive きいて (listening), rather than *kīte*.

Other Points to Note

There are three common cases where *kana* usage is distinctly irregular. They all involve particles, namely the topic particle *wa,* the object particle *o,* and the directional particle *e* (meaning "to"). These words are written は, を, and へ respectively, and not わ, お, and え as might be expected. The irregularities result from the failure of writing conventions to keep pace with pronunciation changes over the last century or so.

Certain further usages need to be noted with regard to *katakana* loan words only. These are relatively recent attempts to express non-Japanese words with greater accuracy, and tend to be an extension of the *yōon* principle (きょ etc.) seen earlier. That is, they combine two *kana* symbols, the first one lending only its consonant sound and this fact being indicated by the small size of the second symbol. For example, "f" sounds can be approximated by following *fu* (フ) with a small vowel. Thus *fa, fi, fe,* and *fo* are written as ファ, フィ, フェ, and フォ respectively. Similarly, "q" can be represented by *ku* (ク) plus a small vowel, as in クォーター (quarter). A German-style "z" (as in "Mozart") can be shown by *tsu* (ツ) plus a small vowel, i.e., モーツァルト (Mozart). "She" (as in "shepherd"), "che" (as in "check"), and the voiced version "je" are written as シェ, チェ and ジェ. Though not a consonant, *u* (ウ) is used in a similar type of combination, to produce "w" sounds. As mentioned earlier, the sounds *wi* and *we* are still occasionally found expressed by ヰ and ヱ respectively, but nowadays are usually written as ウィ and ウェ. Thus "whisky" *(uisukī)* is usually written as ウィスキー. Theoretically ヲ could be used for *wo,* but this has become so associated with the object particle *o* that ウォ is used instead. (*Wa,* however, is represented by ワ.) In similar fashion, *i* (イ) can be followed by a small ェ to express "ye." Thus "Yemen" is イェーメン. Remarkably, an extension of the use of ウ has seen diacritical marks added to it in order to express "v." Thus "Venus" is ヴィーナス. The English sounds "ty" or "ti" (as in "party") and their voiced equivalents "dy" and "di," which were once expressed rather unfaithfully by チ and ジ respectively, are now written as ティ and ディ. Thus "party" is パーティー. The "tu" of "tuba" and the "du" of "due" can be expressed by テュ and デュ, giving テューバ (tuba) and デュエット (duet), while the "Tou" of "Toulouse" can be shown by トゥ (a voiced version is also possible).

These combinations have very recently received official approval, particularly when used in proper nouns such as place names and personal names. However, there is also official recognition of established usage, such as of *b* for *v*. This means that in practice some words can be written in a number of ways. "Violin" can be either ヴァイオリン or バイオリン, for example. In cases where a certain usage has become particularly firmly entrenched in the Japanese language the old rendition is favored, such as ミルクセーキ (mirukusēki) for "milkshake" (but note that "Shakespeare" is シェークスピア). At the same time, it is also possible to make up new combinations as appropriate, such as ニ *(ni)* plus a small ェ *(e)* to express the *nye* sound of the Russian *nyet*. In short, the student should be prepared for a range of creative and sometimes inconsistent usages.

Katakana is very occasionally used for words other than loan words. For example, it can be used to emphasize or highlight words, such as entries in academic reference works, and is also used in telegrams and certain military and official documents. In such cases, when used for purely Japanese or Chinese-derived words, its conventions of usage are identical to those of *hiragana*. Long vowels, for instance, are formed by adding the appropriate vowel and not by a bar. Thus *gakkō* (school) is ガッコウ, rather than ガッコー.

A *kana* symbol can be repeated by the special symbol ゝ. This can also be used when the second symbol is a voiced version of the first, in which case it becomes ゞ. Where more than one syllable is repeated, in vertical script only, 〱 (or 〲 if the first of the repeated sounds is voiced) can be used, with the symbol covering two spaces. These repetition symbols are known collectively as *odoriji* (jump symbols). Students need to recognize them, but should only use them, if at all, with caution. They are not compulsory, and have a number of restrictions on their usage. For example, they cannot be used where the first symbol of one word is the same as the last symbol of the word that precedes it (as in *kuroi ishi* meaning "black stone"), or similarly in compound words where the first symbol of the second word coincides with the last symbol of the first word (as in *tama-matsuri* meaning "festival of the dead"), or where the first symbol of a variable word ending is the same as the last symbol of the word stem (as in ***ki-kimasu*** meaning "listen"). Some examples of correct usage:

みゝ	かゞみ	いろ〱	さま〲
mimi	*kagami*	*iroiro*	*samazama*
(ear)	(mirror)	(various)	(various)

Finally, students should learn the basic Japanese punctuation marks, known as *kutōten*. Full stops are written 。 *(maru)*, and commas are written 、 *(ten)*. Quotation marks *(kagi)*, are written 「 」 in horizontal script and ﹁ ﹂ in vertical script.

I

HIRAGANA

ORIGIN (AN 223)

安	あ	あ	あ

STROKE ORDER

一	ナ	あ	

1 2 3

あ

a

as "a" in "car," but shorter

PRACTICE

あ	あ	あ	あ	あ	あ	あ	あ	あ	あ

ORIGIN (I 419)

以	い	い	い

STROKE ORDER

し	い		

1 2

い

i

as "ee" in "meet," but shorter

PRACTICE

い	い	い	い	い					

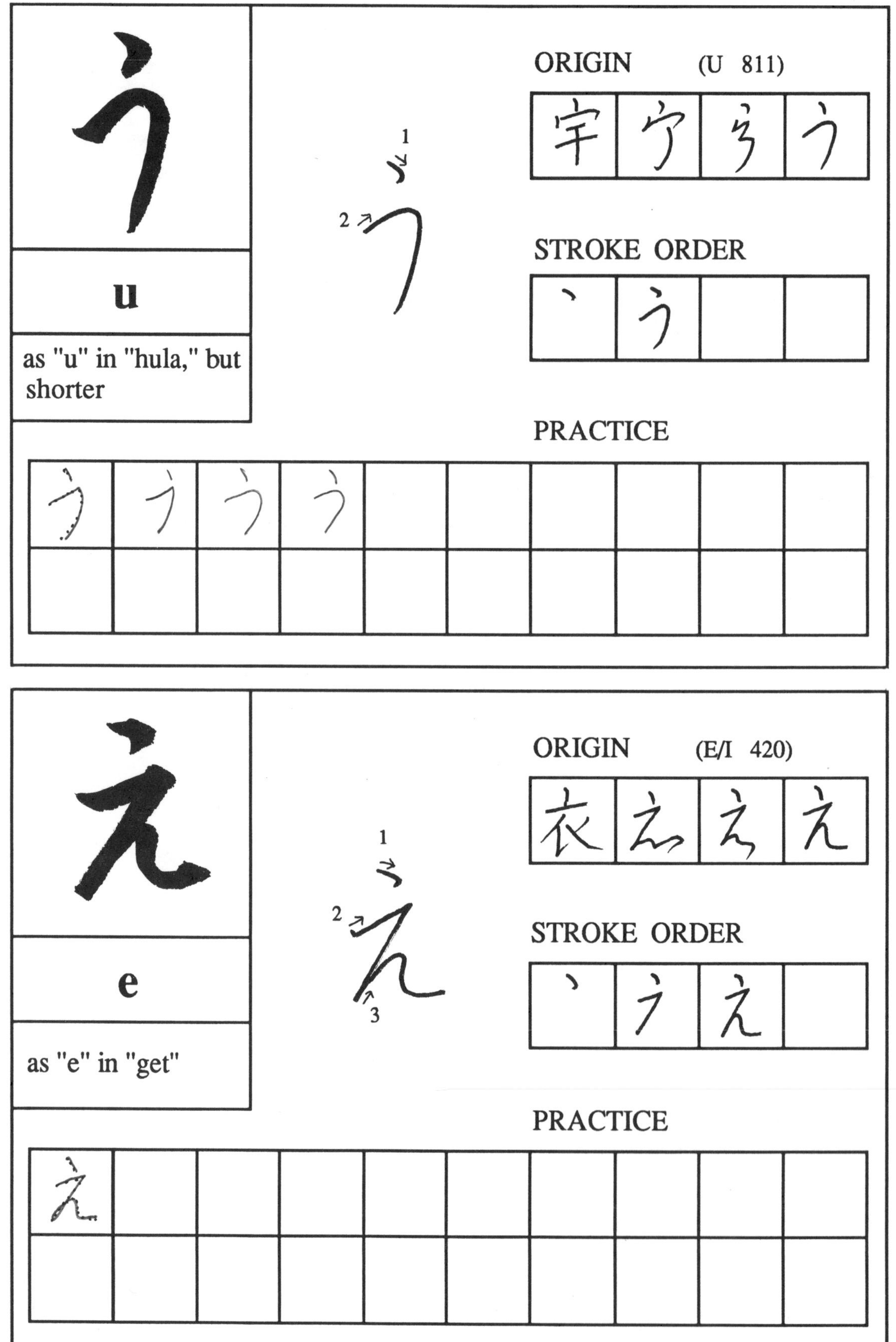
う
u
as "u" in "hula," but shorter
ORIGIN (U 811)
宇
1
2
STROKE ORDER
PRACTICE
え
e
as "e" in "get"
ORIGIN (E/I 420)
衣
1
2
3
STROKE ORDER
PRACTICE

ORIGIN (O)

於	(cursive)	(cursive)	お

STROKE ORDER

一	あ	お	

お

o

as "o" in "or," but shorter

PRACTICE

ORIGIN (KA 431)

加	(cursive)	(cursive)	か

STROKE ORDER

つ	カ	か	

か

ka

as "ca" in "car," but shorter

PRACTICE

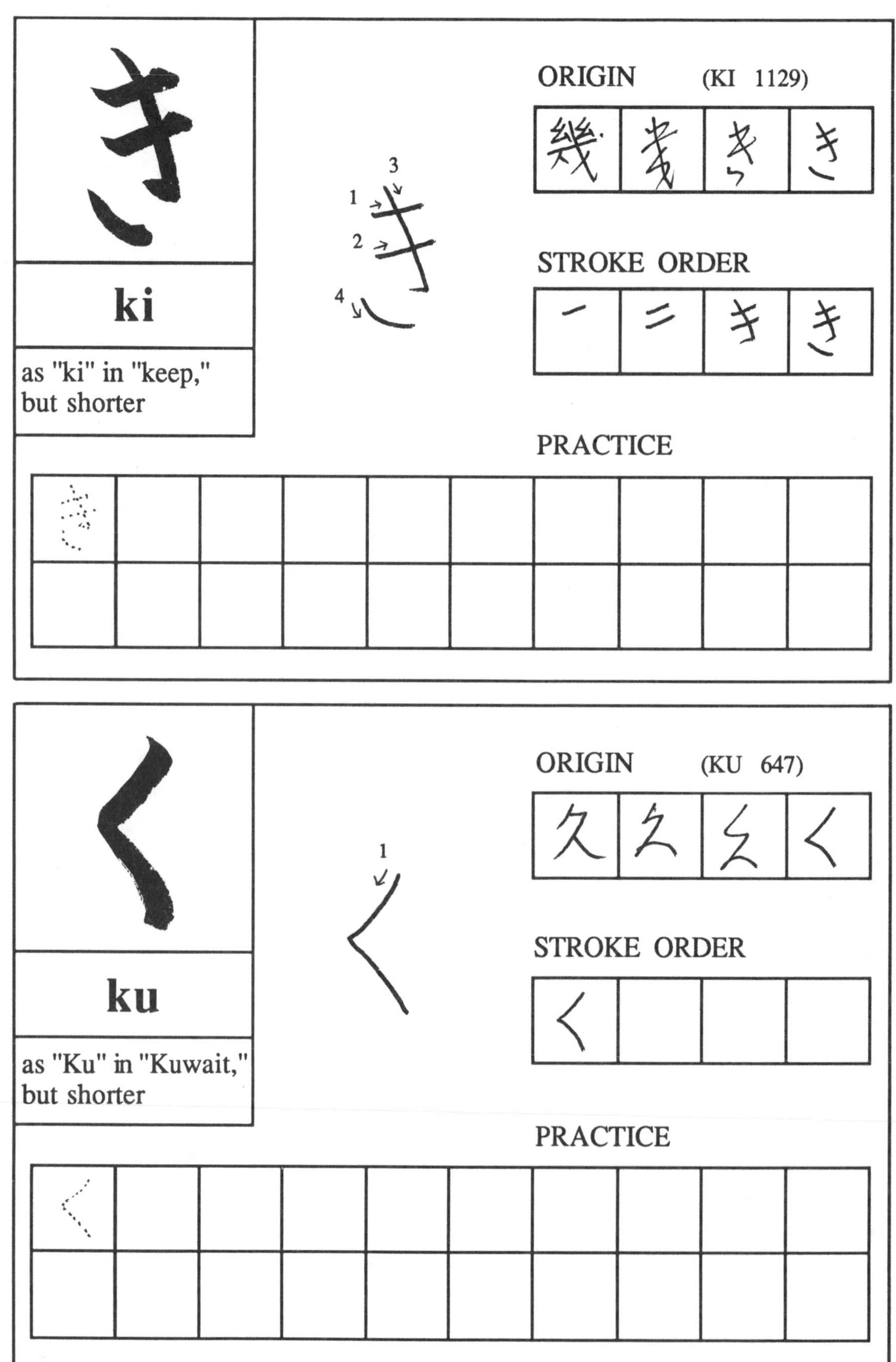

き
ki
as "ki" in "keep," but shorter
ORIGIN (KI 1129)
幾
STROKE ORDER
PRACTICE
く
ku
as "Ku" in "Kuwait," but shorter
ORIGIN (KU 647)
久
STROKE ORDER
PRACTICE

け

ke

as "ke" in "keg"

ORIGIN (KEI 105)

計	计	け	け

STROKE ORDER

1 2 3

PRACTICE

こ

ko

as "co" in "core," but shorter

ORIGIN (KO 855)

己	己	乙	こ

STROKE ORDER

1 2

PRACTICE

MINI REVIEW あ — こ / *A — KO*

あい	***ai***	love
うえ	***ue***	above, top
おか	***oka***	hill
きく	***kiku***	hear, ask; chrysanthemum
こけ	***koke***	moss
いけ	***ike***	pond
かう	***kau***	buy
えき	***eki***	station
いく	***iku***	go
ここ	***koko***	here
あう	***au***	meet

koe voice

こえ

kaku write

かく

oke wooden bucket

おけ

kao face, honor

かお

ie house, extended family

いえ

aki autumn

あき

iu say

いう

akai red

あかい

aoi blue

あおい

kioku memory

きおく

ekaki painter

えかき

さ

sa

as "sa" in "sarcasm," but shorter

ORIGIN (SA 22)

左			さ

STROKE ORDER

PRACTICE

し

shi

as "shee" in "sheep," but shorter

ORIGIN (SHI, part of 1335)

之			し

STROKE ORDER

し			

PRACTICE

ORIGIN (SUN 909)

寸	す	す	す

STROKE ORDER

一	す		

1 2

す

su

as "Su" in "Susan," but shorter

PRACTICE

ORIGIN (SE 327)

世	せ	せ	せ

STROKE ORDER

一	十	せ	

1 2 3

せ

se

as "se" in "set"

PRACTICE

そ

so

as "so" in "sore," but shorter

ORIGIN (SO, part of ZŌ 741)

曾

STROKE ORDER

PRACTICE

た

ta

as "ta" in "tar," but shorter

ORIGIN (TA 164)

太

STROKE ORDER

PRACTICE

ORIGIN (CHI 169)

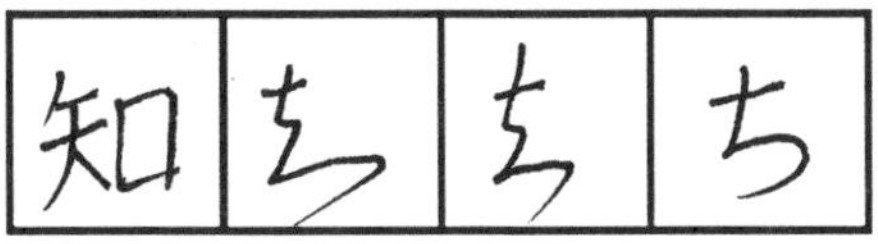

知	ち	ち	ち

STROKE ORDER

一	ち		

1 2

ち

PRACTICE

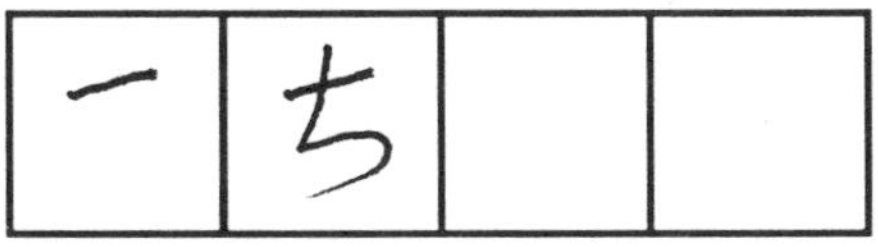

ち

chi

as "chee" in "cheek," but shorter

ORIGIN (SU 304)

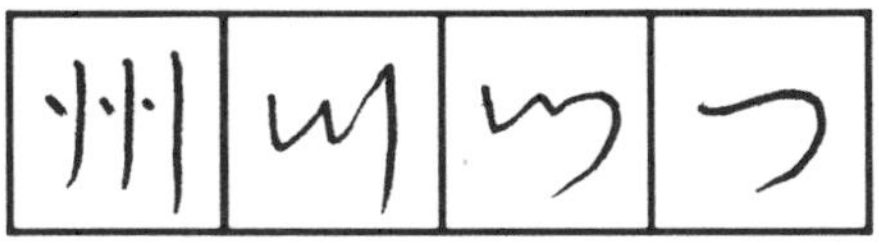

州	川	つ	つ

STROKE ORDER

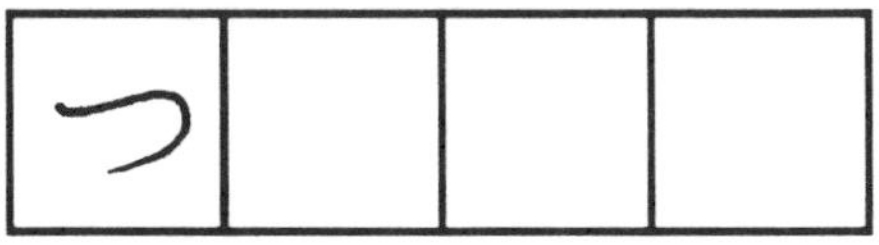

つ			

1

つ

PRACTICE

つ

tsu

as "tsu" in "tsunami"

て

te

as "te" in "ten"

ORIGIN (TEN 58)

天	云	て	て

STROKE ORDER

て			

PRACTICE

と

to

as "to" in "tore," but shorter

ORIGIN (TO-maru 129)

止	止	と	と

STROKE ORDER

ヽ	と		

PRACTICE

MINI REVIEW さ — と / *SA — TO*

romaji	meaning	hiragana
sushi	sushi	すし
tsuchi	soil	つち
soto	outside	そと
sake	saké; salmon	さけ
tetsu	iron, steel	てつ
seki	seat; cough	せき
tatsu	stand, leave; dragon	たつ
tochi	land	とち
uta	song, poem	うた
koto	thing; Japanese harp	こと
suso	hem	すそ

tai	sea bream
たい	
teki	enemy
てき	
shichi	seven
しち	
ase	sweat
あせ	
sasu	thrust; indicate
さす	
uso	untruth
うそ	
kisetsu	season
きせつ	
ashita	tomorrow
あした	
satoi	clever, sharp (of senses)
さとい	
sekitei	rock garden (Japanese style)
せきてい	
chikatetsu	subway
ちかてつ	

ORIGIN (NA)

奈			な

STROKE ORDER

na

as "na" in "narcotic," but shorter

PRACTICE

ORIGIN (NI 906)

仁		に	に

STROKE ORDER

ni

as "nea" in "neat," but shorter

PRACTICE

ぬ

nu

as "noo" in "noon," but shorter

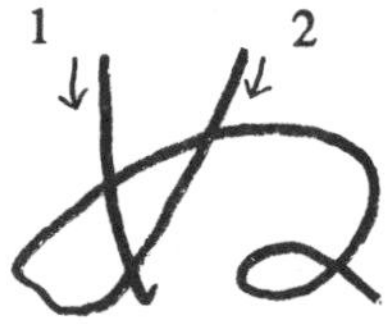

ORIGIN (NU/DO 1638)

奴	ぬ	ぬ	ぬ

STROKE ORDER

ｌ	ぬ		

PRACTICE

ね

ne

as "ne" in "net"

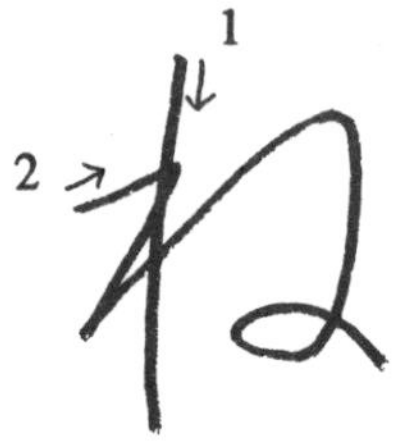

ORIGIN (NE)

禰	ね	ね	ね

STROKE ORDER

ｌ	ね		

PRACTICE

ORIGIN (NO/NAI)

乃	乃	乃	の

STROKE ORDER

の			

の 1

の

no

as "no" in "north," but shorter

PRACTICE

の									

ORIGIN (HA 367)

波	波	は	は

STROKE ORDER

し	に	は	

は 1 2 3

は

ha

as "ha" in "harm," but shorter

PRACTICE

は									

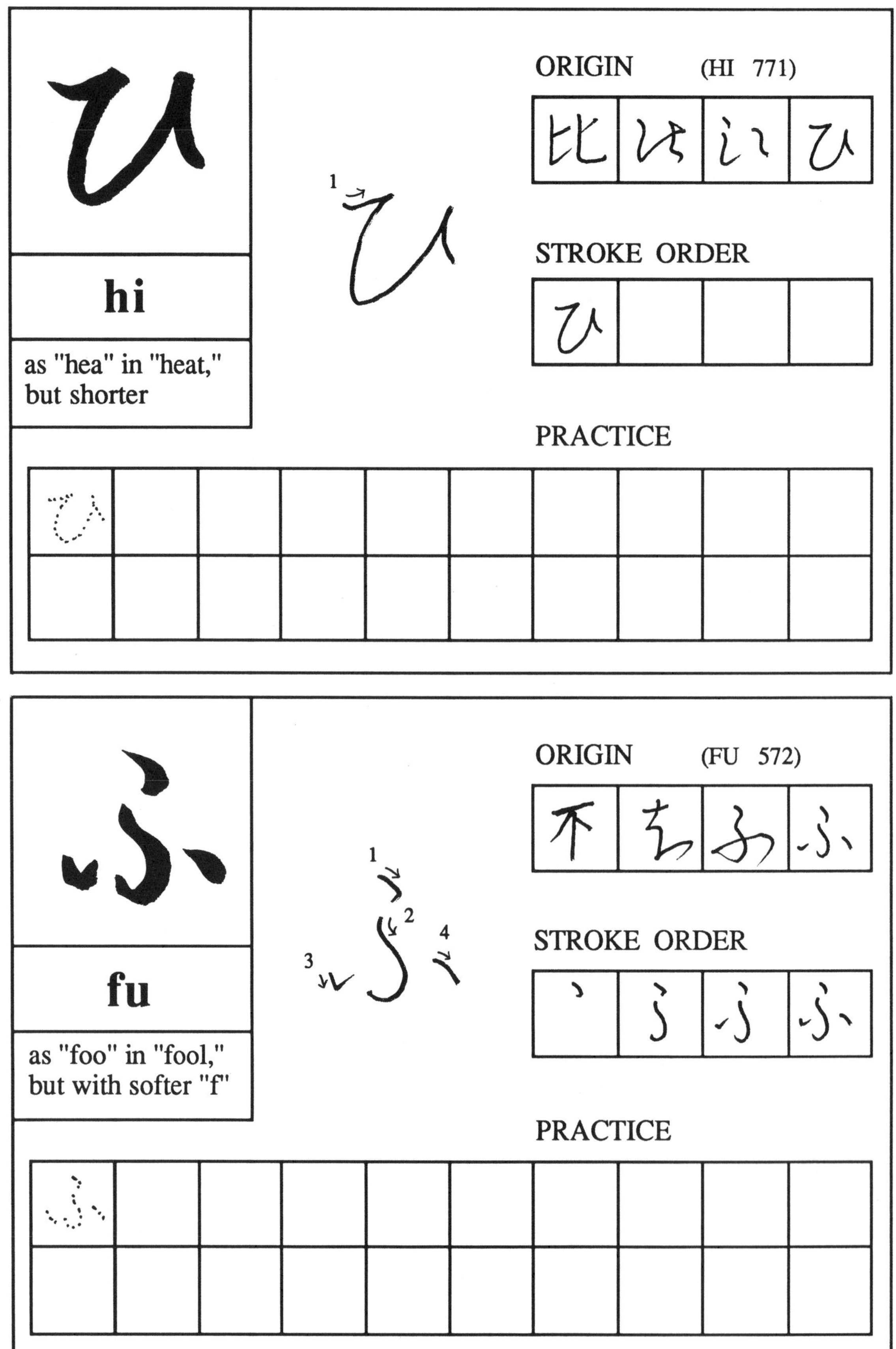
ひ
hi
as "hea" in "heat," but shorter
ORIGIN (HI 771)
比
STROKE ORDER
PRACTICE
ふ
fu
as "foo" in "fool," but with softer "f"
ORIGIN (FU 572)
不
STROKE ORDER
PRACTICE

ORIGIN (HE/BU 384)

部	ろ	つ	へ

STROKE ORDER

へ			

PRACTICE

へ

he

as "he" in "hen"

ORIGIN (HO 787)

保	𛃁	ほ	ほ

STROKE ORDER

し	に	に	ほ

PRACTICE

ほ

ho

as "ho" in "horn," but shorter

MINI REVIEW な — ほ / *NA — HO*

nani	what
なに	
hone	bone
ほね	
nuno	cloth
ぬの	
hifu	skin
ひふ	
heta	clumsy
へた	
hana	flower, blossom; nose
はな	
fune	boat
ふね	
kani	crab
かに	
hina	doll, fledgling
ひな	
hashi	chopsticks; bridge; edge
はし	
kinu	silk
きぬ	

hoshi star

ほし

hito person

ひと

noki eaves

のき

nishi west

にし

haiku haiku

はいく

katana curved sword

かたな

netsuke carved figurine

ねつけ

tanuki raccoon dog

たぬき

seifu government

せいふ

inoshishi wild boar

いのしし

heisotsu soldier

へいそつ

ま

ma

as "ma" in "mark," but shorter

ま (1, 2, 3)

ORIGIN (MATSU 587)

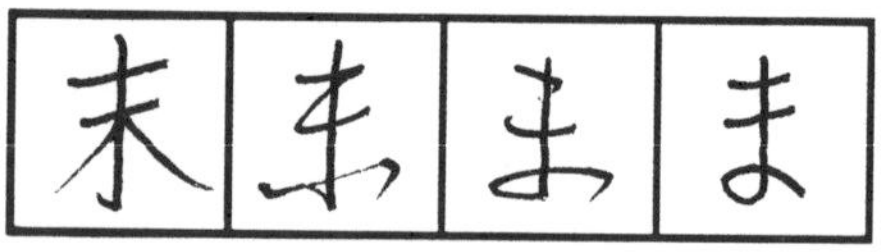

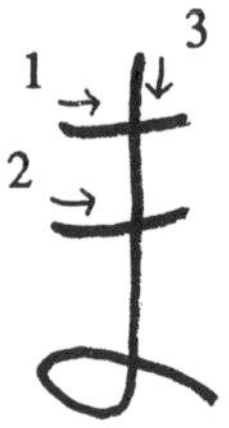

末	末	ま	ま

STROKE ORDER

一	二	ま	

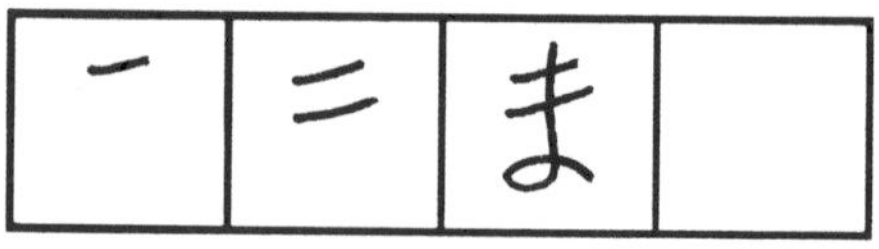

PRACTICE

み

mi

as "mea" in "meat," but shorter

み (1, 2)

ORIGIN (BI 376)

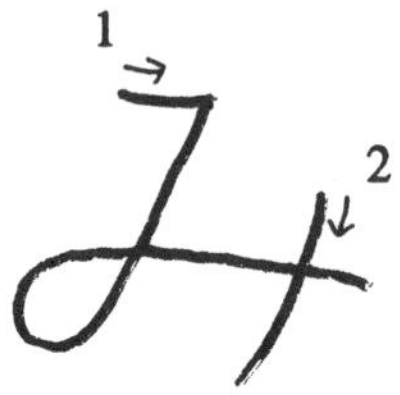

美	美	み	み

STROKE ORDER

み	み		

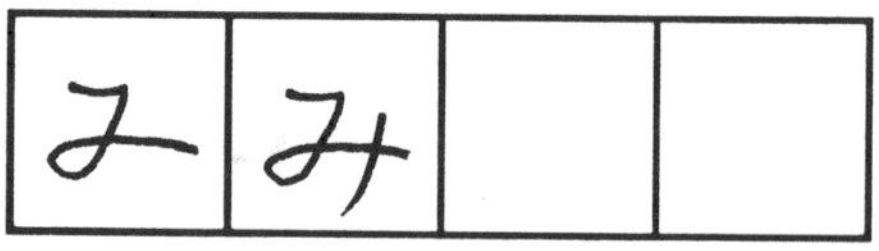

PRACTICE

ORIGIN (MU 781)

武	𛁈	む	む

STROKE ORDER

一	む	む	

む

1 2 3

む

mu

as "moo" in "moon," but shorter

PRACTICE

む									

ORIGIN (ME 35)

女	女	め	め

STROKE ORDER

㇏	め		

め

1 2

め

me

as "me" in "met"

PRACTICE

め									

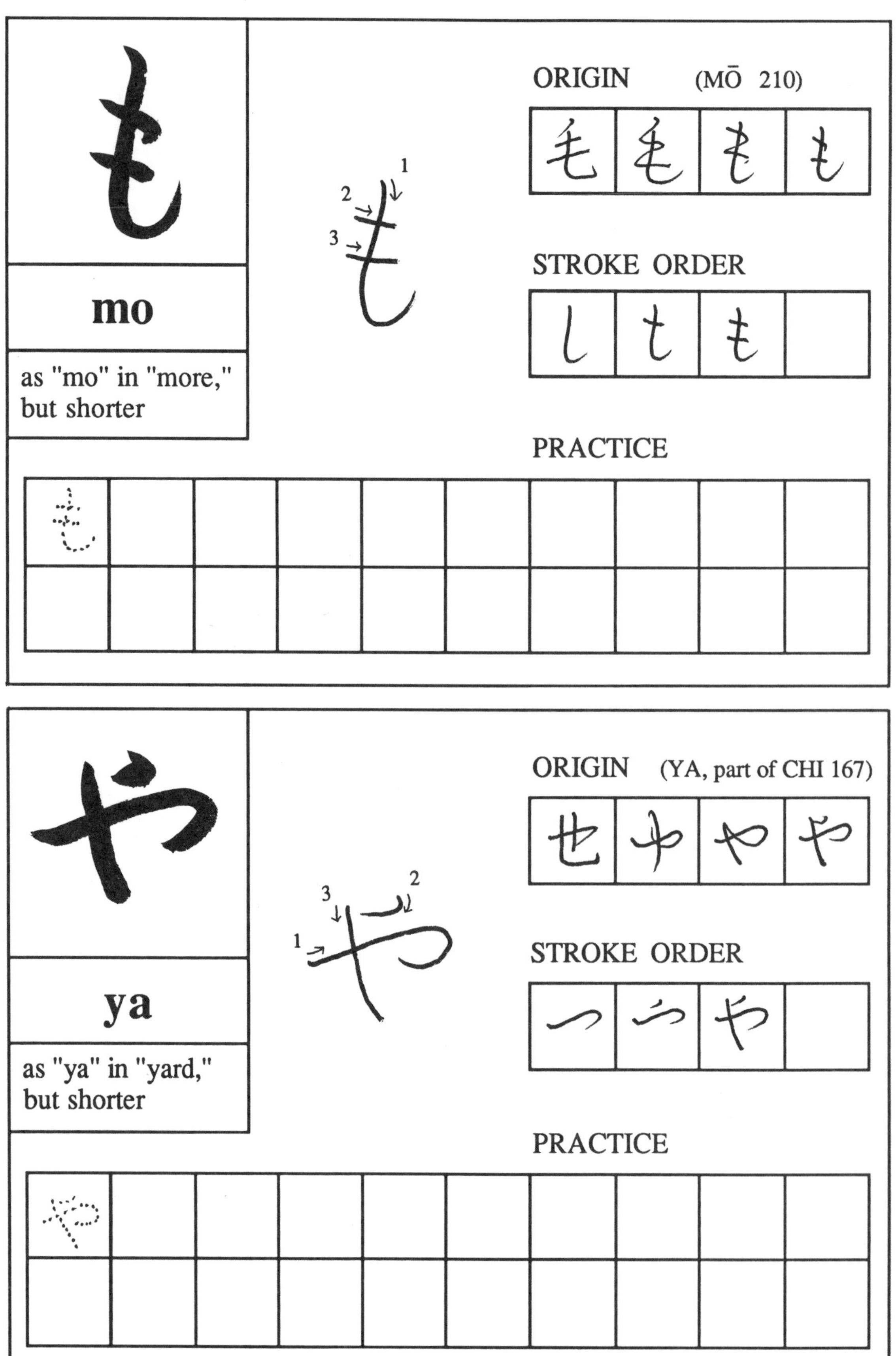
も
mo
as "mo" in "more," but shorter
1
2
3
ORIGIN (MŌ 210)
毛
STROKE ORDER
PRACTICE
や
ya
as "ya" in "yard," but shorter
1
2
3
ORIGIN (YA, part of CHI 167)
也
STROKE ORDER
PRACTICE

ORIGIN (YU 399)

由			

STROKE ORDER

	ゆ		

ゆ

yu

as "you" in "youth," but shorter

PRACTICE

ORIGIN (YO 1873)

与			よ

STROKE ORDER

	よ		

よ

yo

as "Yo" in "York," but shorter

PRACTICE

MINI REVIEW ま — よ / *MA — YO*

	romaji	meaning
やま	*yama*	mountain, hill
ゆめ	*yume*	dream
よむ	*yomu*	read
もも	*momo*	peach
みや	*miya*	shrine
こめ	*kome*	uncooked rice
つゆ	*tsuyu*	dew
むし	*mushi*	insect
まつ	*matsu*	pine; wait
うめ	*ume*	Japanese plum
むね	*mune*	chest, breast

kimono	kimono, clothing
きもの	
sashimi	sliced raw fish
さしみ	
Yamato	old name for Japan
やまと	
yukata	cotton kimono
ゆかた	
sumie	India-ink drawing
すみえ	
emaki	picture scroll
えまき	
hanami	blossom viewing
はなみ	
mikoshi	portable shrine
みこし	
ukiyoe	woodblock print
うきよえ	
setomono	porcelain
せともの	
sukiyaki	sukiyaki
すきやき	

ら

ra

as "ra" in "mirage," but shorter

ORIGIN (RA/RYŌ 598)

良	ら	ら	ら

STROKE ORDER

ヽ	ら		

PRACTICE

り

ri

as "ree" in "reek," but shorter

ORIGIN (RI 596)

利	わ	り	り

STROKE ORDER

ｌ	り		

PRACTICE

ORIGIN (RU 805)

留		る	る

STROKE ORDER

る			

1

る

ru

as "ru" in "rule," but shorter

PRACTICE

ORIGIN (REI 413)

礼			れ

STROKE ORDER

	れ		

1

2

れ

re

as "re" in "red"

PRACTICE

ろ

ro

as "ro" in "roar," but shorter

ORIGIN (RO 256)

呂			ろ

1

STROKE ORDER

ろ			

PRACTICE

わ

wa

as "wa" in "watt"

ORIGIN (WA 416)

和			わ

1 2

STROKE ORDER

	わ		

PRACTICE

ORIGIN (ON/EN 79)

遠			を

STROKE ORDER

1 2 3

PRACTICE

を

o

as "o" in "or," but shorter

ORIGIN (MU)

无			ん

STROKE ORDER

1

PRACTICE

ん

n

as "n" in "sin"

MINI REVIEW ら — ん / *RA — N*

wan	bowl; bay
わん	
tera	temple
てら	
tsuru	crane; to fish
つる	
kore	this
これ	
furo	bath
ふろ	
nori	edible seaweed; paste
のり	
haru	spring; to stretch
はる	
rei	politeness; soul; example
れい	
shiro	castle; white
しろ	
Nihon	Japan
にほん	
sakura	cherry blossom
さくら	

uchiwa round fan

うちわ

matsuri festival

まつり

hotaru firefly

ほたる

futon futon

ふとん

rekishi history

れきし

wafuku Japanese clothing

わふく

riron theory

りろん

furoshiki cloth wrapper for parcels

ふろしき

harakiri harakiri

はらきり

Hinomaru Rising Sun Flag

ひのまる

samurai samurai

さむらい

VOICED AND HALF-VOICED SOUNDS

ga as "ga" in "garden" but shorter

が

gi as "gee" in "geese" but shorter

ぎ

gu as "goo" in "goose" but shorter

ぐ

ge as "ge" in "get"

げ

go as "go" in "gore" but shorter

ご

za as "za" in "bizarre" but shorter

ざ

ji as "jee" in "jeep" but shorter

じ

zu as "zoo" but shorter

ず

ze as "ze" in "zest"

ぜ

zo as "zo" in "Azores" but shorter

ぞ

da as "da" in "dark" but shorter

だ													

ji as "jee" in "jeep" but shorter

ぢ													

zu as "zoo" but shorter

づ													

de as "de" in "desk"

で													

do as "doo" in "door" but shorter

ど													

ba as "ba" in "bark" but shorter

ば						

pa as "pa" in "park" but shorter

ぱ						

bi as "bea" in "beak" but shorter

び						

pi as "pea" in "peak" but shorter

ぴ						

bu as "boo" in "boot" but shorter

ぶ						

pu as "poo" in "pool" but shorter

ぷ						

be as "be" in "beg"

べ						

pe as "pe" in "peg"

ぺ						

bo as "bo" in "bore" but shorter

ぼ						

po as "po" in "pork" but shorter

ぽ						

REVIEW OF VOICED AND HALF-VOICED SOUNDS

Romaji	Hiragana	Meaning
obi	おび	waist sash for kimono
fude	ふで	writing brush
Zen	ぜん	Zen
soba	そば	buckwheat noodles; side
biwa	びわ	lute; loquat
geta	げた	wooden clogs
Obon	おぼん	Buddhist festival
Kabuki	かぶき	Kabuki drama
ojigi	おじぎ	bow (head)
sanpo	さんぽ	walk, stroll
monpe	もんぺ	old-style work pants

keigo polite language

けいご

mikado old word for emperor

みかど

manga cartoon

まんが

mikuji written oracle

みくじ

yakuza gangster

やくざ

nigiri rice ball

にぎり

tengu long-nosed goblin

てんぐ

hanaji nosebleed

はなぢ

mizuwari whisky and water

みずわり

zonjiru know, believe

ぞんじる

daibutsu large statue of Buddha

だいぶつ

kamikaze kamikaze

かみかぜ									

origami origami

おりがみ									

senpai senior

せんぱい									

bonsai bonsai

ぼんさい									

ikebana ikebana

いけばな									

enpitsu pencil

えんぴつ									

yokozuna sumo grand champion

よこづな									

tenpura tempura

てんぷら									

senbei rice cracker

せんべい									

hanafuda flower cards (game)

はなふだ									

Fujisan Mt. Fuji

ふじさん									

REVIEW OF DOUBLE VOWELS AND CONSONANTS

Kana	Romanization	Meaning
ああ	*ā (aa)*	like that; Oh!
いい	*ii*	good
ええ	*ē (ee)*	yes
くう	*kū*	sky, void, nothingness
くう	*kuu*	eat
とお	*tō*	ten
とう	*tō*	tower, pagoda
とう	*tou*	ask
かっぱ	*kappa*	mythical creature
しっき	*shikki*	lacquerware
すもう	*sumō*	sumo

zōri sandals

そうり

sūji numeral

すうじ

yūgen tranquil beauty

ゆうげん

gakkō school

がっこう

kōyō red leaves

こうよう

ōkii big

おおきい

kendō kendo

けんどう

jingū shrine

じんぐう

fūrin wind chime

ふうりん

shintō Shinto

しんとう

kūkō airport

くうこう

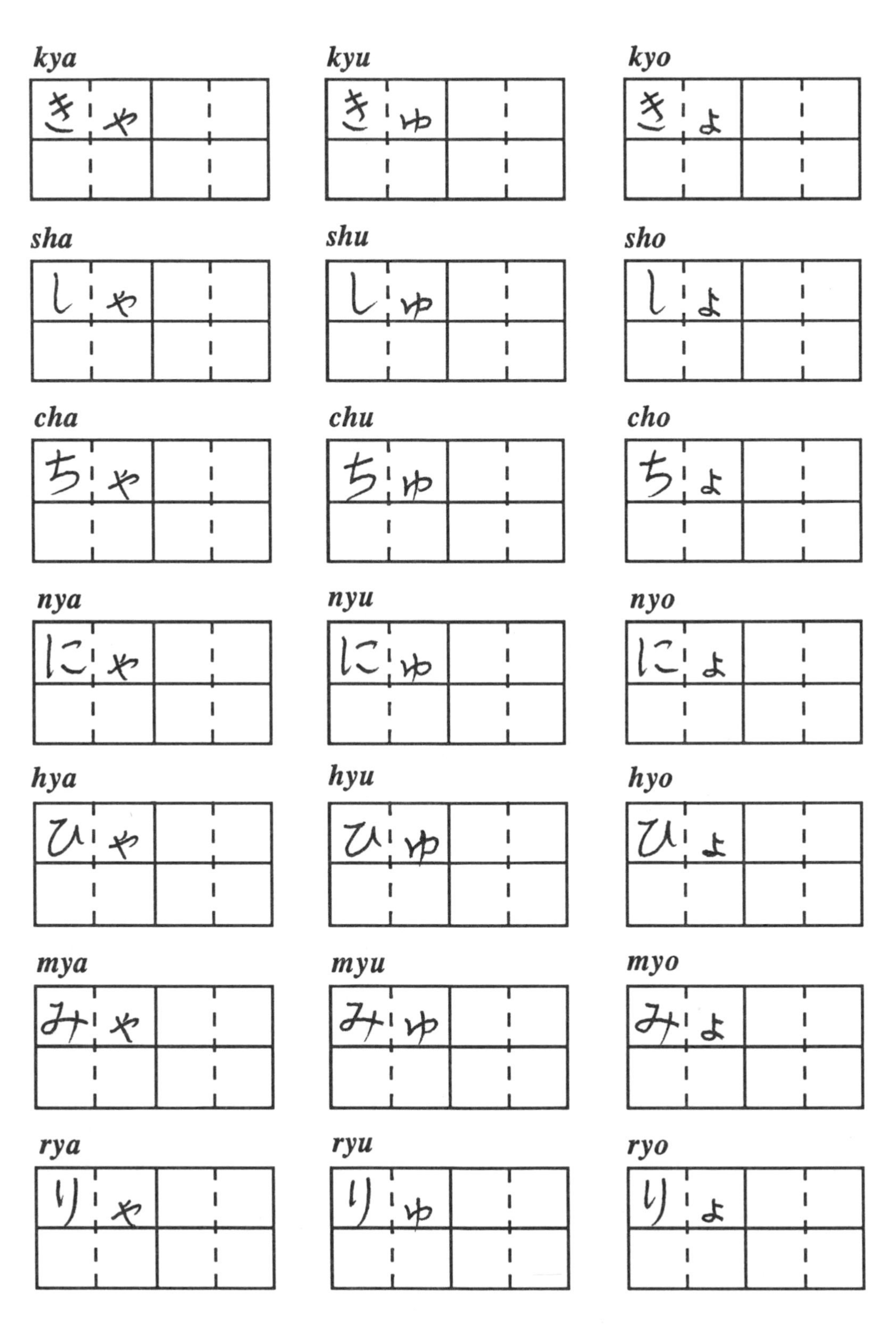
COMBINED SOUNDS KYA—RYO / きゃ — りょ
kya
きゃ
kyu
きゅ
kyo
きょ
sha
しゃ
shu
しゅ
sho
しょ
cha
ちゃ
chu
ちゅ
cho
ちょ
nya
にゃ
nyu
にゅ
nyo
にょ
hya
ひゃ
hyu
ひゅ
hyo
ひょ
mya
みゃ
myu
みゅ
myo
みょ
rya
りゃ
ryu
りゅ
ryo
りょ

VOICED COMBINED SOUNDS *GYA—BYO* / ぎゃ — びょ

gya

ぎゃ

gyu

ぎゅ

gyo

ぎょ

ja

じゃ

ju

じゅ

jo

じょ

ja

ぢゃ

ju

ぢゅ

jo

ぢょ

bya

びゃ

byu

びゅ

byo

びょ

HALF-VOICED COMBINED SOUNDS *PYA—PYO* / ぴゃ — ぴょ

pya

ぴゃ

pyu

ぴゅ

pyo

ぴょ

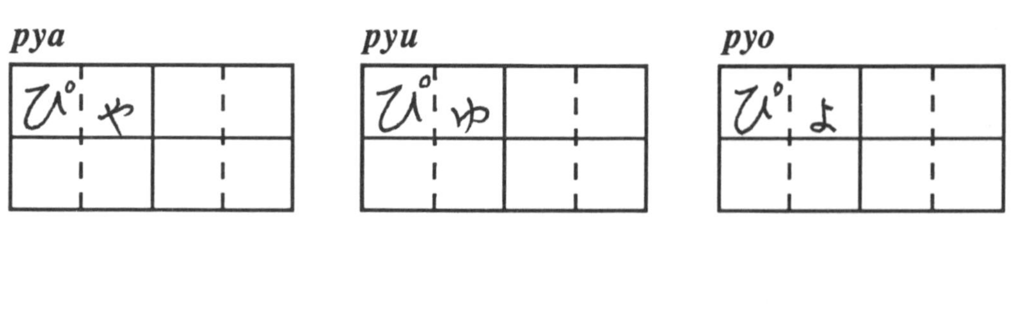

REVIEW OF COMBINED SOUNDS

kyaku guest, visitor

きゃく

shōji sliding screen

しょうじ

byōbu folding screen

びょうぶ

jinja shrine

じんじゃ

chanoyu tea ceremony

ちゃのゆ

geisha geisha

げいしゃ

shodō calligraphy

しょどう

yakyū baseball

やきゅう

enryo reserve, restraint

えんりょ

myōji family name

みょうじ

kingyo goldfish

きんぎょ

nyūshi entrance examination

にゅうし

Jukyō Confucianism

じゅきょう

chōchin paper lantern

ちょうちん

hyōzan iceberg

ひょうざん

ryūgaku overseas study

りゅうがく

kōjō factory

こうじょう

jūdō judo

じゅうどう

Bukkyō Buddhism

ぶっきょう

shōgun shogun

しょうぐん

nyōbō wife

にょうぼう

happyō announcement

はっぴょう

REVIEW THROUGH PLACE NAMES AND PERIOD NAMES

Nara place, period 710 - 794

なら

Edo place, period 1603 - 1868

えど

Kōbe place

こうべ

Yayoi period c. 250 B.C. - c. A.D. 250

やよい

Ginza place

ぎんざ

Hakone place

はこね

Meiji period 1868 - 1912

めいじ

Nagoya place

なごや

Matsushima place

まつしま

Heian period 794 - 1185

へいあん

Shōwa period 1926 - 1989

しょうわ

Nikkō place

にっこう											

Sapporo place

さっぽろ											

Ōsaka place

おおさか											

Kyōto place

きょうと											

Muromachi period 1392 - 1573

むろまち											

Heisei period 1989 -

へいせい											

Kamakura period 1185 - 1333

かまくら											

Honshū place

ほんしゅう														

Taishō period 1912 - 1926

たいしょう														

Jōmon period c. 8000 - c. 250 B.C.

じょうもん														

Tōkyō place

とうきょう														

GENERAL REVIEW

Romanization	Meaning	Hiragana
Nō	Noh	のう
sabi	elegant simplicity; rust	さび
semi	cicada	せみ
giri	duty, honor	ぎり
tako	kite; octopus	たこ
hakama	divided skirt	はかま
urushi	lacquer	うるし
honne	one's real intent	ほんね
kokeshi	stylized wooden doll	こけし
haniwa	clay figurine	はにわ
udon	wheat noodles	うどん

kotatsu brazier, footwarmer

こたつ

amae childlike dependence

あまえ

Ebisu name of god of wealth

えびす

miai interview for marriage

みあい

tōfu tofu

とうふ

seibo year-end gift

せいぼ

shibumi astringency

しぶみ

aware pathos

あわれ

gohan meal, cooked rice

ごはん

gagaku ancient court music

ががく

noren shop curtain

のれん

haori short coat

はおり

meishi name card

めいし

odori dance

おどり

kaisha company

かいしゃ

menboku reputation, "face"

めんぼく

shinju pearl

しんじゅ

mugicha barley tea

むぎちゃ

tennō emperor

てんのう

shōgi Japanese chess

しょうぎ

onsen hot spring

おんせん

misoshiru miso soup

みそしる

ninja	ninja
にんじゃ	
tokonoma	decorative alcove
とこのま	
soroban	abacus
そろばん	
bunraku	puppet theater
ぶんらく	
bentō	box lunch
べんとう	
dantai	group
だんたい	
shamisen	samisen
しゃみせん	
Shōgatsu	New Year
しょうがつ	
shakuhachi	flute
しゃくはち	
koinobori	carp streamer
こいのぼり	
janken	"scissors-paper-stone" game
じゃんけん	

II

KATAKANA

ORIGIN (A)

阿	阝	ア	ア

STROKE ORDER

フ	ア		

ア

a

as "a" in "car," but shorter

PRACTICE

ORIGIN (I)

伊	イ		

STROKE ORDER

ノ	イ		

イ

i

as "ee" in "meet," but shorter

PRACTICE

ウ

u

as "u" in "hula," but shorter

ORIGIN (U 811)

宇			ウ

STROKE ORDER

PRACTICE

エ

e

as "e" in "get"

ORIGIN (E 1244)

江			エ

STROKE ORDER

PRACTICE

ORIGIN (O)

於	方	オ	オ

STROKE ORDER

一	ナ	オ	

1 2 3 オ

オ

o

as "o" in "or," but shorter

PRACTICE

オ									

ORIGIN (KA 431)

加	か	カ	カ

STROKE ORDER

フ	カ		

1 2 カ

カ

ka

as "ca" in "car," but shorter

PRACTICE

カ									

キ

ki

as "ki" in "keep," but shorter

ORIGIN (KI 1129)

幾	き	き	キ

STROKE ORDER

一	二	キ	

PRACTICE

ク

ku

as "Ku" in "Kuwait," but shorter

ORIGIN (KU 647)

久	久	ク	ク

STROKE ORDER

ノ	ク		

PRACTICE

ORIGIN (KAI 1059)

介	介	ケ	ケ

STROKE ORDER

ノ	ノ	ケ	

1 2 3

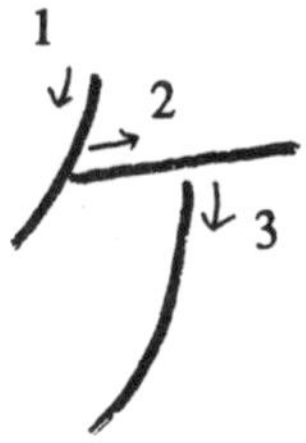

ケ

ke

as "ke" in "keg"

PRACTICE

ケ

ORIGIN (KO 855)

己	己	コ	コ

STROKE ORDER

フ	コ		

1 2

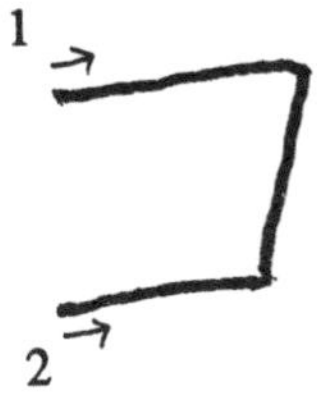

コ

ko

as "co" in "core," but shorter

PRACTICE

コ

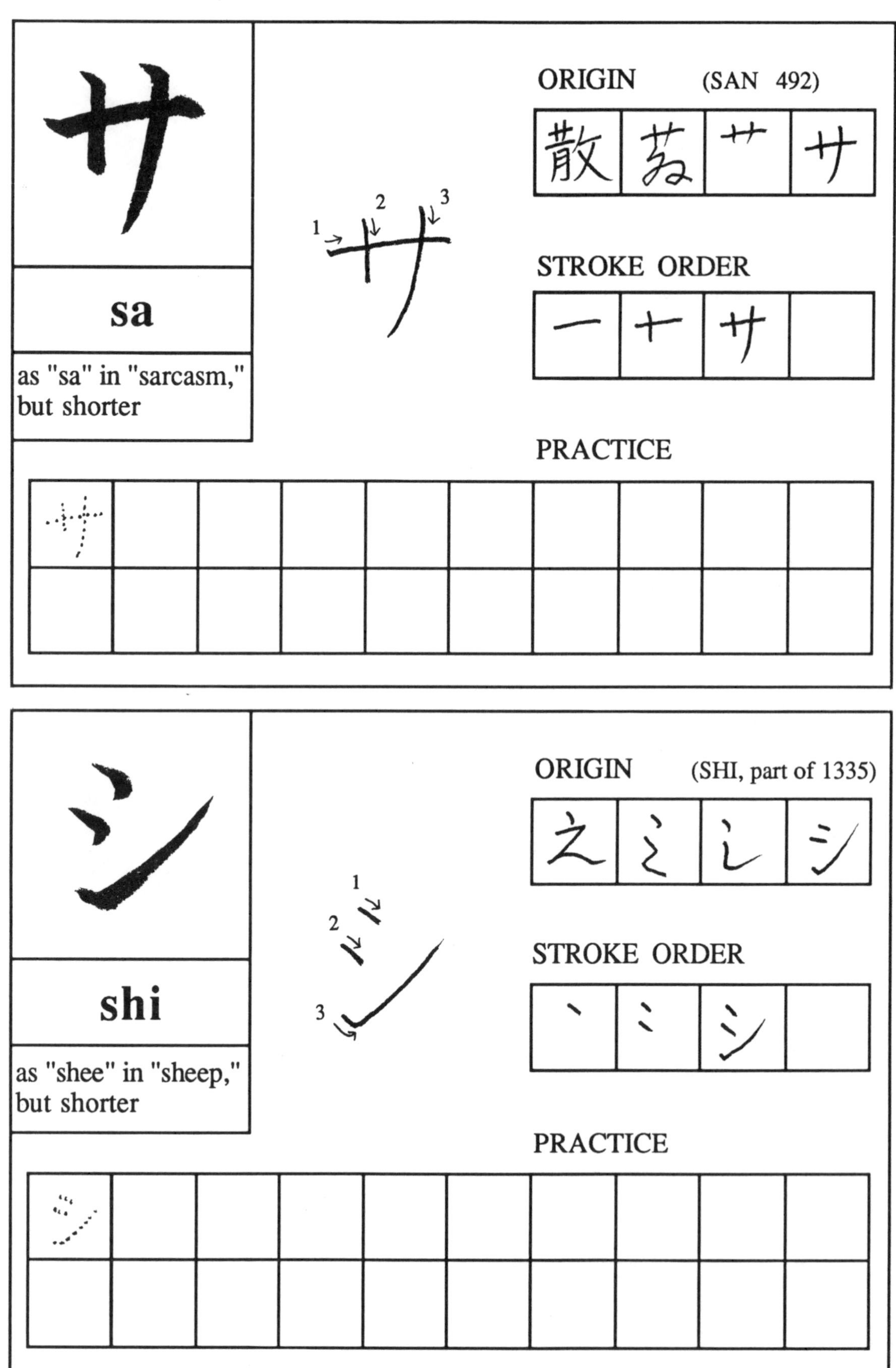
サ
sa
as "sa" in "sarcasm," but shorter
ORIGIN (SAN 492)
散
STROKE ORDER
PRACTICE
シ
shi
as "shee" in "sheep," but shorter
ORIGIN (SHI, part of 1335)
之
STROKE ORDER
PRACTICE

ORIGIN (SU)

須	须	ス	ス

STROKE ORDER

フ	ス		

1 2

ス

su

as "Su" in "Susan," but shorter

PRACTICE

ス									

ORIGIN (SE 327)

世	せ	セ	セ

STROKE ORDER

一	セ		

2 1

セ

se

as "se" in "set"

PRACTICE

セ									

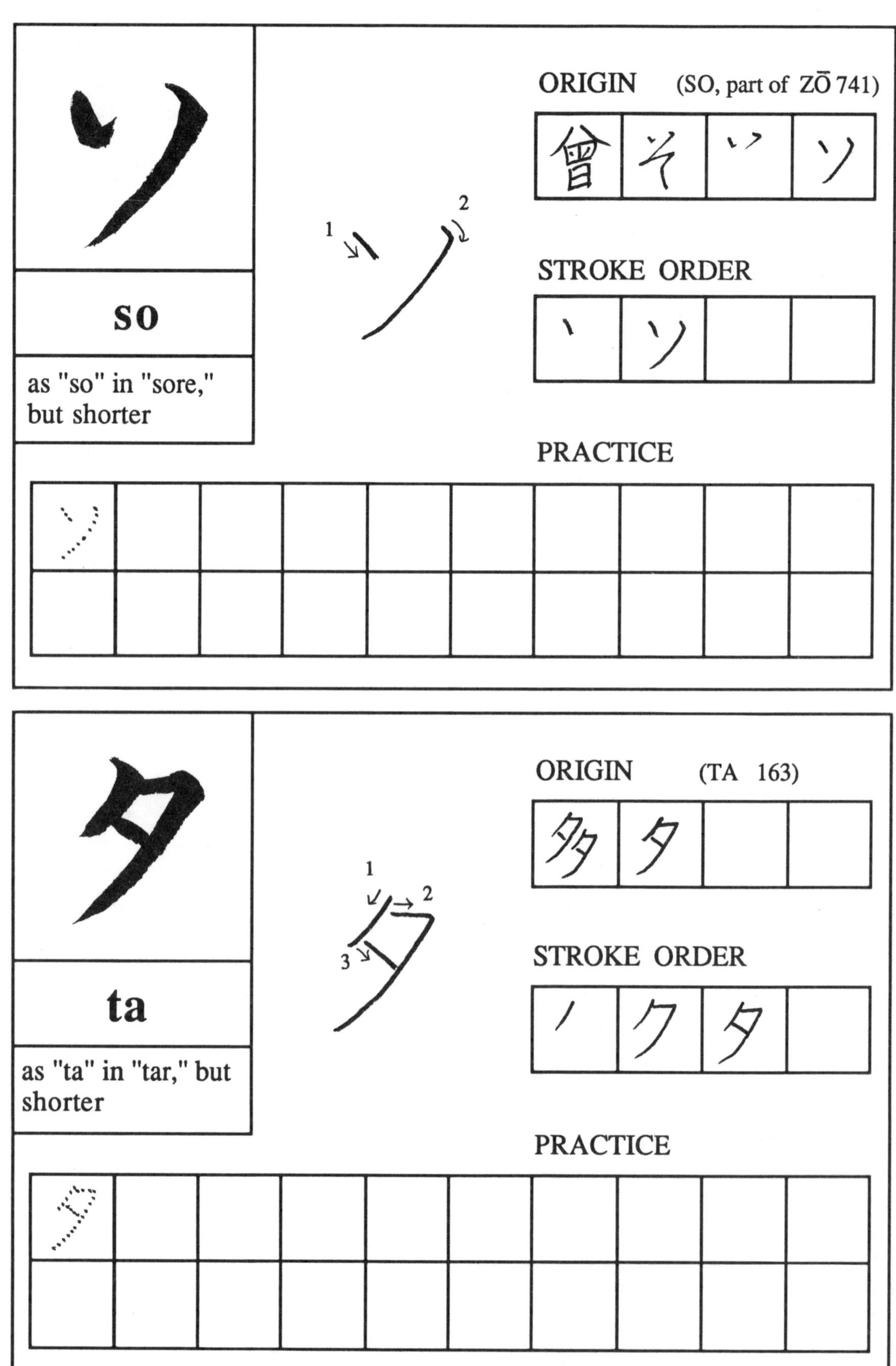
ソ
so
as "so" in "sore," but shorter
1
2
ORIGIN (SO, part of ZŌ 741)
曾
STROKE ORDER
PRACTICE
タ
ta
as "ta" in "tar," but shorter
1
2
3
ORIGIN (TA 163)
多
タ
STROKE ORDER
PRACTICE

ORIGIN (CHI 47)

千	チ		

STROKE ORDER

ノ	二	チ	

1 2 3 チ

チ

chi

as "chee" in "cheek," but shorter

PRACTICE

ORIGIN (SU 304)

州			ツ

STROKE ORDER

丶	丶丶	ツ	

1 2 3 ツ

ツ

tsu

as "tsu" in "tsunami"

PRACTICE

テ

te

as "te" in "ten"

ORIGIN (TEN 58)

天	天	天	テ

STROKE ORDER

一	二	テ	

PRACTICE

ト

to

as "to" in "tore," but shorter

ORIGIN (TO-maru 129)

止	上	ト	ト

STROKE ORDER

丨	ト		

PRACTICE

MINI REVIEW ア — ト / *A — TO*

katsu	cutlet
カツ	
aisu	ice
アイス	
ēsu	ace
エース	
kēki	cake
ケーキ	
auto	out (baseball)
アウト	
sāchi	search
サーチ	
kōto	coat; court (sports)
コート	
tsuā	tour
ツアー	
tesuto	test
テスト	
shītsu	sheet (bed)
シーツ	
sekuto	sect
セクト	

kōchi coach (sports)

コ	ー	チ												

sōsu sauce

ソ	ー	ス												

sukī ski, skiing

ス	キ	ー												

takushī taxi

タ	ク	シ	ー								

sutēki steak

ス	テ	ー	キ								

sētā sweater

セ	ー	タ	ー								

sākasu circus

サ	ー	カ	ス								

ōkē okay

オ	ー	ケ	ー								

ēkā acre

エ	ー	カ	ー								

akashia acacia

ア	カ	シ	ア								

sukēto skate, skating

ス	ケ	ー	ト								

ORIGIN (NA)

奈	大	ナ	

STROKE ORDER

一	ナ		

1 2

ナ

na

as "na" in "narcotic," but shorter

PRACTICE

ORIGIN (NI 61)

二	二		

STROKE ORDER

一	二		

1 2

ニ

ni

as "nea" in "neat," but shorter

PRACTICE

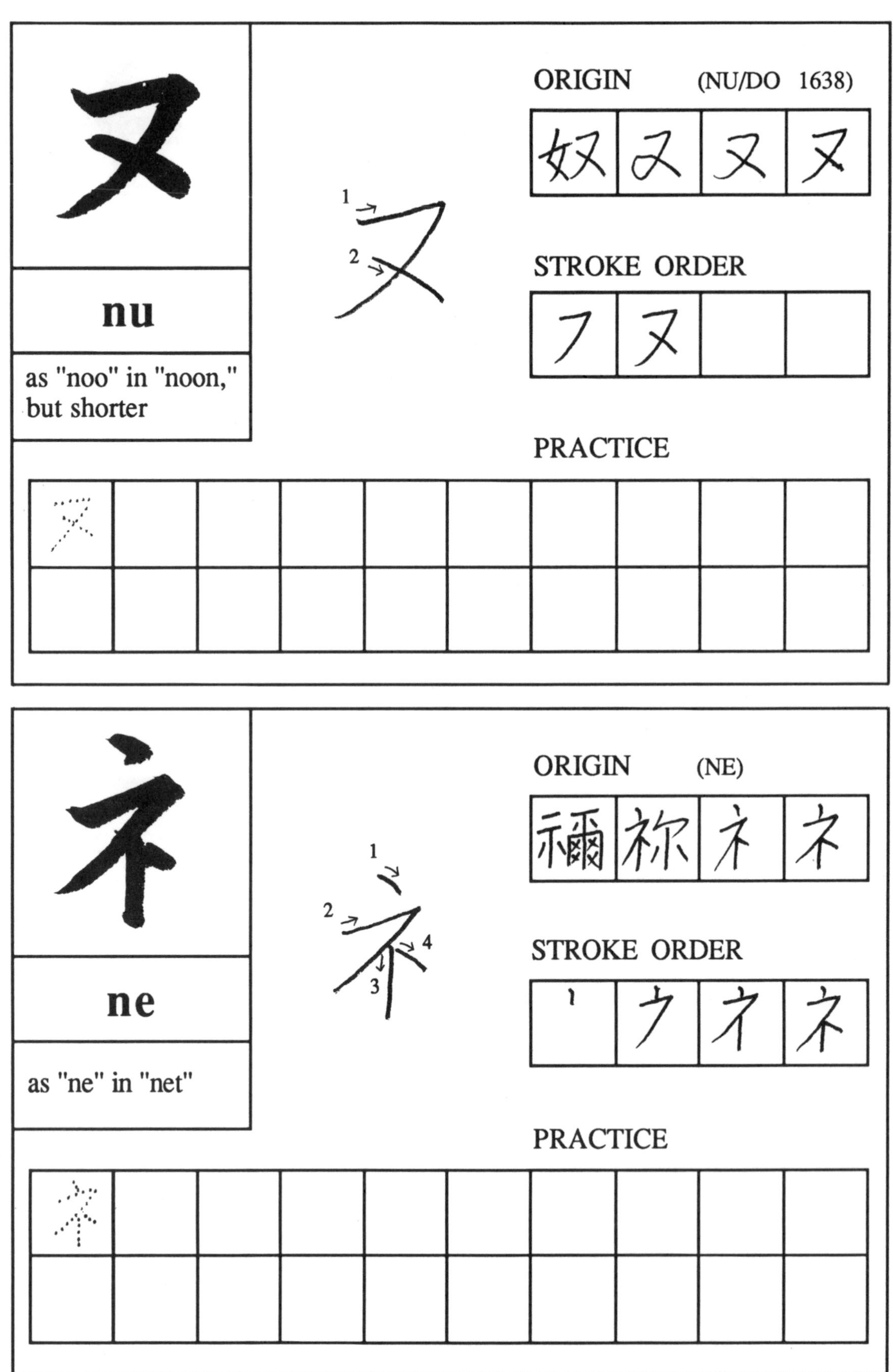
ヌ
ORIGIN (NU/DO 1638)
奴
STROKE ORDER
nu
as "noo" in "noon," but shorter
PRACTICE
ネ
ORIGIN (NE)
禰 祢
STROKE ORDER
ne
as "ne" in "net"
PRACTICE

ORIGIN (NO/NAI)

乃	ノ		

STROKE ORDER

ノ			

1

ノ

ノ

no

as "no" in "north," but shorter

PRACTICE

ORIGIN (HACHI 66)

八	ハ		

STROKE ORDER

ノ	ハ		

1 2

ハ

ハ

ha

as "ha" in "harm," but shorter

PRACTICE

ヒ

hi

as "hea" in "heat," but shorter

ORIGIN (HI 771)

比	ひ	ヒ	ヒ

STROKE ORDER

一	ヒ		

PRACTICE

フ

fu

as "foo" in "fool," but with softer "f"

ORIGIN (FU 572)

不	ア	フ	

STROKE ORDER

フ			

PRACTICE

ORIGIN (HE/BU 384)

部	ろ	へ	へ

STROKE ORDER

へ			

1

PRACTICE

he

as "he" in "hen"

ORIGIN (HO 787)

保	呆	ホ	

STROKE ORDER

一	十	才	ホ

2 1 3 4

PRACTICE

ho

as "ho" in "horn," but shorter

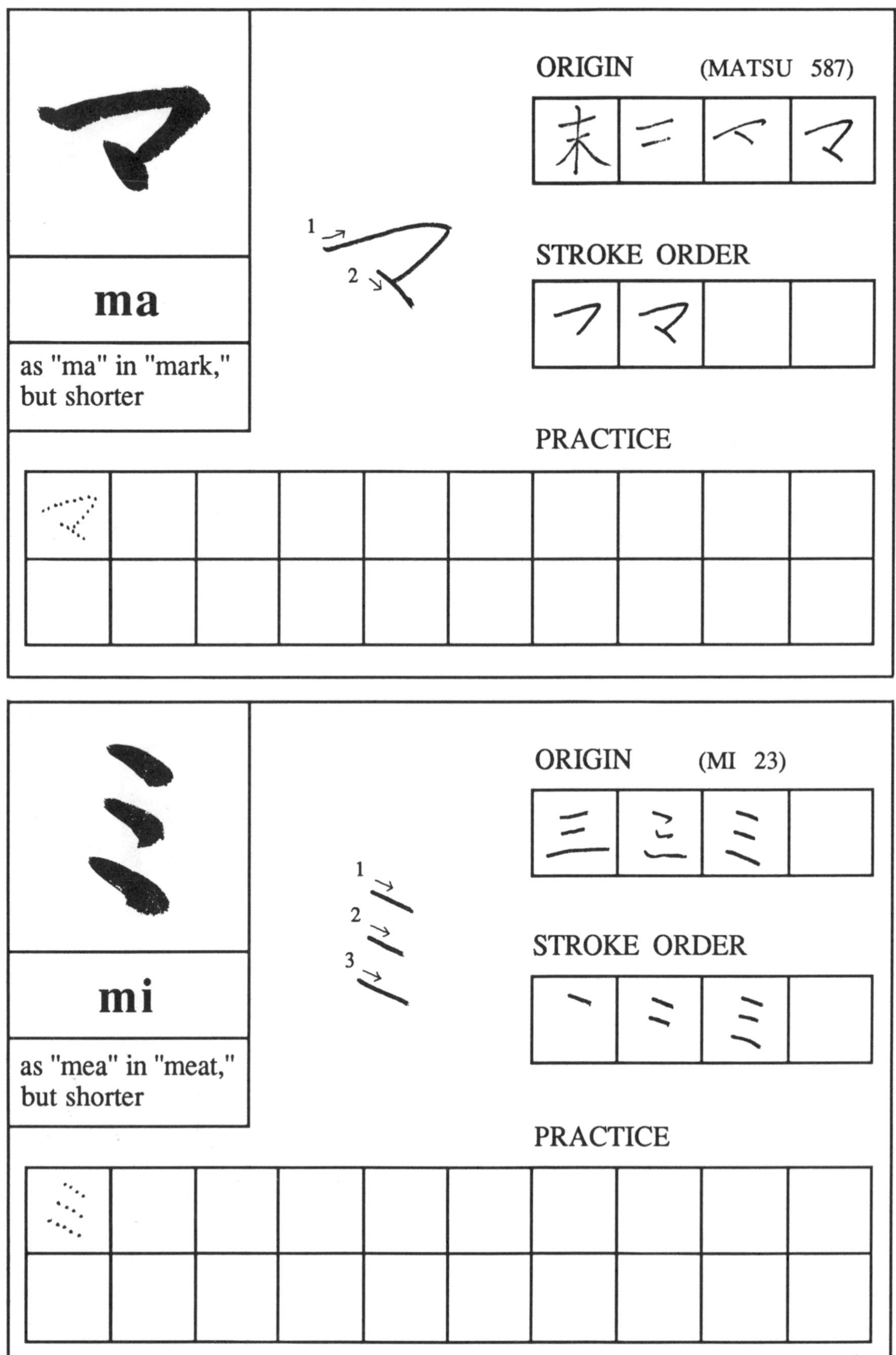
ORIGIN (MATSU 587)
末
STROKE ORDER
ma
as "ma" in "mark," but shorter
PRACTICE
ORIGIN (MI 23)
三
STROKE ORDER
mi
as "mea" in "meat," but shorter
PRACTICE

ORIGIN (MU)

牟	ム	ム	

STROKE ORDER

ム	ム		

1 2

ム

mu

as "moo" in "moon," but shorter

PRACTICE

ム

ORIGIN (ME 35)

女	女	メ	メ

STROKE ORDER

ノ	メ		

1 2

メ

me

as "me" in "met"

PRACTICE

メ

モ

mo

as "mo" in "more," but shorter

ORIGIN (MŌ 210)

毛	モ	モ	モ

STROKE ORDER

一	二	モ	

PRACTICE

ヤ

ya

as "ya" in "yard," but shorter

ORIGIN (YA, part of CHI 167)

也	ヤ	ヤ	ヤ

STROKE ORDER

フ	ヤ		

PRACTICE

ORIGIN (YU 399)

由	ユ	ユ	

STROKE ORDER

フ	ユ		

ユ

yu

as "you" in "youth," but shorter

PRACTICE

ORIGIN (YO 1873)

与	ヨ	ヨ	ヨ

STROKE ORDER

フ	ヨ	ヨ	

ヨ

yo

as "Yo" in "York," but shorter

PRACTICE

ラ

ra

as "ra" in "mirage," but shorter

1 2

ORIGIN (RA/RYŌ 598)

良	ラ	ラ	ラ

STROKE ORDER

一	ラ		

PRACTICE

リ

ri

as "ree" in "reek," but shorter

1 2

ORIGIN (RI 596)

利	リ	リ	

STROKE ORDER

ｌ	リ		

PRACTICE

ORIGIN (RU 409)

流	ル	ル	ル

STROKE ORDER

ノ	ル		

1 2
ル

ル

ru

as "ru" in "rule," but shorter

PRACTICE

ORIGIN (REI 413)

礼	レ	レ	レ

STROKE ORDER

レ			

1
レ

レ

re

as "re" in "red"

PRACTICE

ロ

ro

as "ro" in "roar," but shorter

ORIGIN (RO 256)

呂	ロ	ロ	

STROKE ORDER

丨	冂	ロ	

PRACTICE

ワ

wa

as "wa" in "watt"

ORIGIN (WA 416)

和	ロ	ワ	ワ

STROKE ORDER

丨	ワ		

PRACTICE

ORIGIN (KO, part of 856)

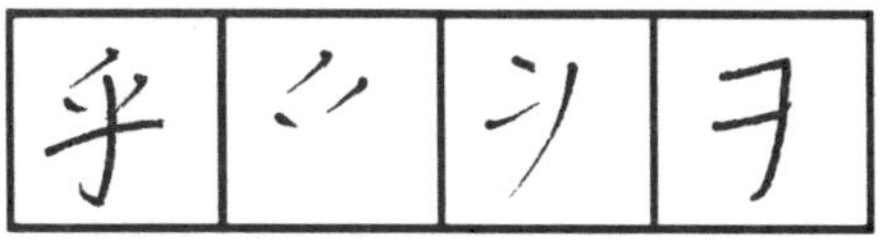

乎			ヲ

STROKE ORDER

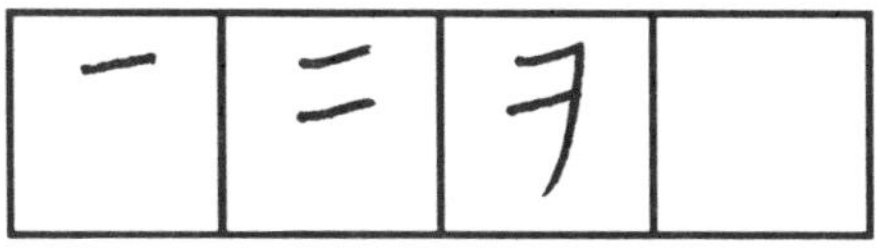

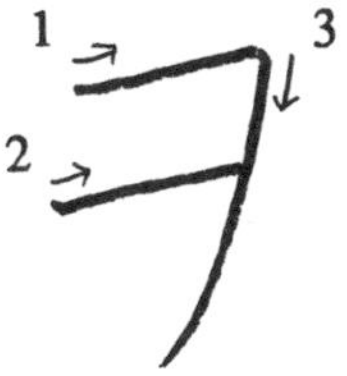

		ヲ	

PRACTICE

ヲ

o

as "o" in "or," but shorter

ORIGIN (NI)

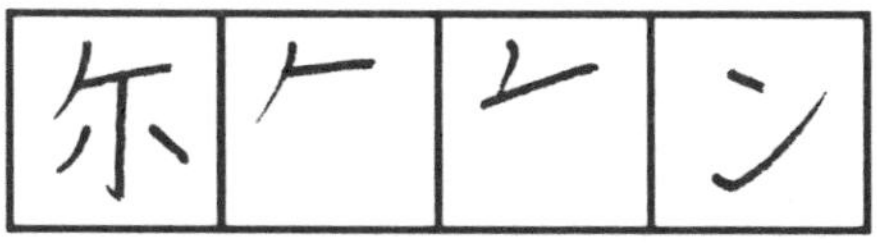

尓			ン

STROKE ORDER

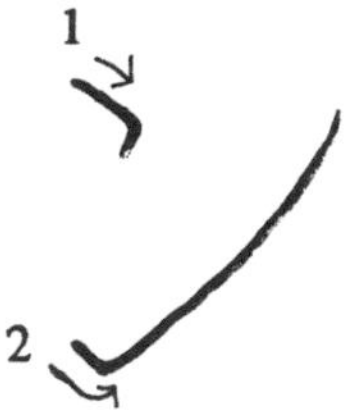

丶	ン		

PRACTICE

ン

n

as "n" in "sin"

MINI REVIEW ナ — ン/*NA — N*

heri	helicopter
ヘリ	
memo	memo
メモ	
hire	fillet
ヒレ	
miruku	milk
ミルク	
kanū	canoe
カヌー	
wanisu	varnish
ワニス	
rōn	loan
ローン	
naifu	knife
ナイフ	
furē	Hooray!
フレー	
nōto	note, notebook
ノート	
taiya	tire (car)
タイヤ	

kamera camera

カメラ

nēmu name, reputation

ネーム

yūmoa humor

ユーモア

mainasu minus

マイナス

sararī salary

サラリー

hanmā hammer

ハンマー

yōyō yoyo

ヨーヨー

hankachi handkerchief

ハンカチ

yunīku unique

ユニーク

nekutai necktie

ネクタイ

hōmuran home run

ホームラン

VOICED AND HALF-VOICED SOUNDS

ga as "ga" in "garden" but shorter

ガ													

gi as "gee" in "geese" but shorter

ギ													

gu as "goo" in "goose" but shorter

グ													

ge as "ge" in "get"

ゲ													

go as "go" in "gore" but shorter

ゴ													

za as "za" in "bizarre" but shorter

ザ													

ji as "jee" in "jeep" but shorter

ジ													

zu as "zoo" but shorter

ズ													

ze as "ze" in "zest"

ゼ													

zo as "zo" in "Azores" but shorter

ゾ													

da as "da" in "dark" but shorter

ダ

ji as "jee" in "jeep" but shorter

ヂ

zu as "zoo" but shorter

ヅ

de as "de" in "desk"

デ

do as "doo" in "door" but shorter

ド

ba as "ba" in "bark" but shorter

バ

pa as "pa" in "park" but shorter

パ

bi as "bea" in "beak" but shorter

ビ

pi as "pea" in "peak" but shorter

ピ

bu as "boo" in "boot" but shorter

ブ

pu as "poo" in "pool" but shorter

プ

be as "be" in "beg"

ベ

pe as "pe" in "peg"

ペ

bo as "bo" in "bore" but shorter

ボ

po as "po" in "pork" but shorter

ポ

REVIEW OF VOICED AND HALF-VOICED SOUNDS

ビル	***biru***	office building
ゼロ	***zero***	zero
バス	***basu***	bus, bath
ギヤ	***giya***	gear
ダンス	***dansu***	dance
ゲーム	***gēmu***	game
ガイド	***gaido***	guide, guidebook
ゴルフ	***gorufu***	golf
ベース	***bēsu***	base
ズボン	***zubon***	trousers
ゴリラ	***gorira***	gorilla

daburu double

ダブル

zōn zone

ゾーン

jiguzagu zigzag

ジグザグ

repōto report

レポート

jīnzu jeans

ジーンズ

wāpuro word processor

ワープロ

pachinko Japanese pinball

パチンコ

dezāto dessert

デザート

pīman green pepper

ピーマン

mai pēsu at one's own speed ("my pace")

マイペース

arubaito part-time job

アルバイト

COMBINED SOUNDS *KYA—RYO* / キャ—リョ

kya
キャ

kyu
キュ

kyo
キョ

sha
シャ

shu
シュ

sho
ショ

cha
チャ

chu
チュ

cho
チョ

nya
ニャ

nyu
ニュ

nyo
ニョ

hya
ヒャ

hyu
ヒュ

hyo
ヒョ

mya
ミャ

myu
ミュ

myo
ミョ

rya
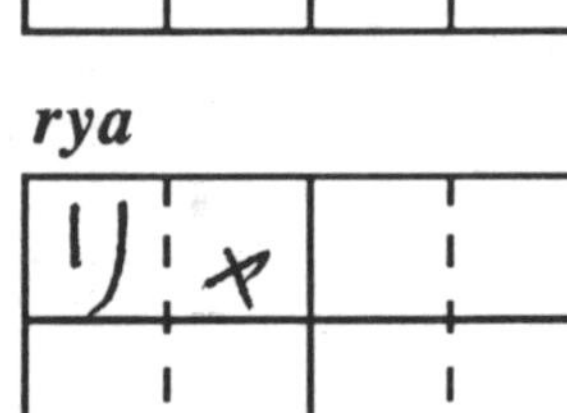

ryu
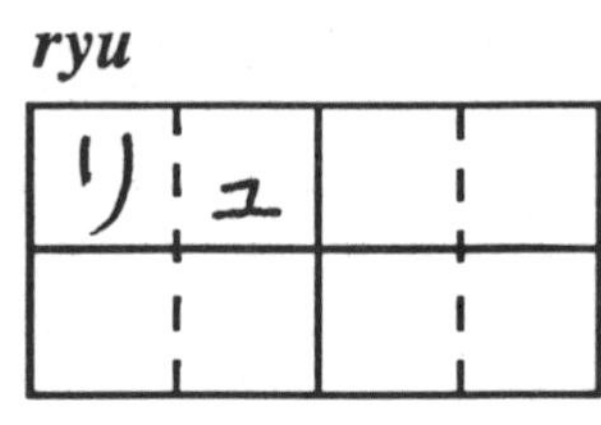

ryo
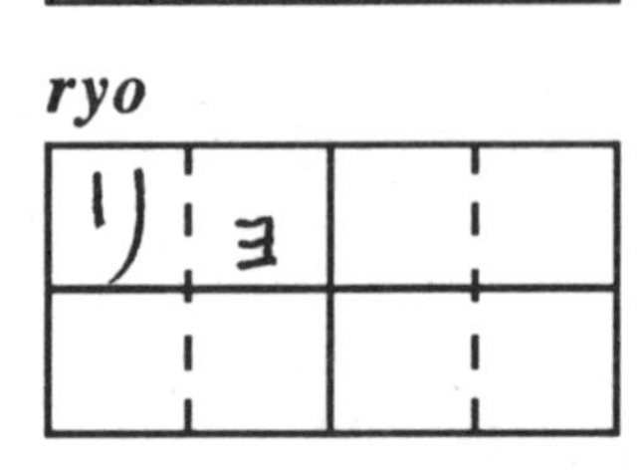

VOICED COMBINED SOUNDS *GYA—BYO* / ギャ—ビョ

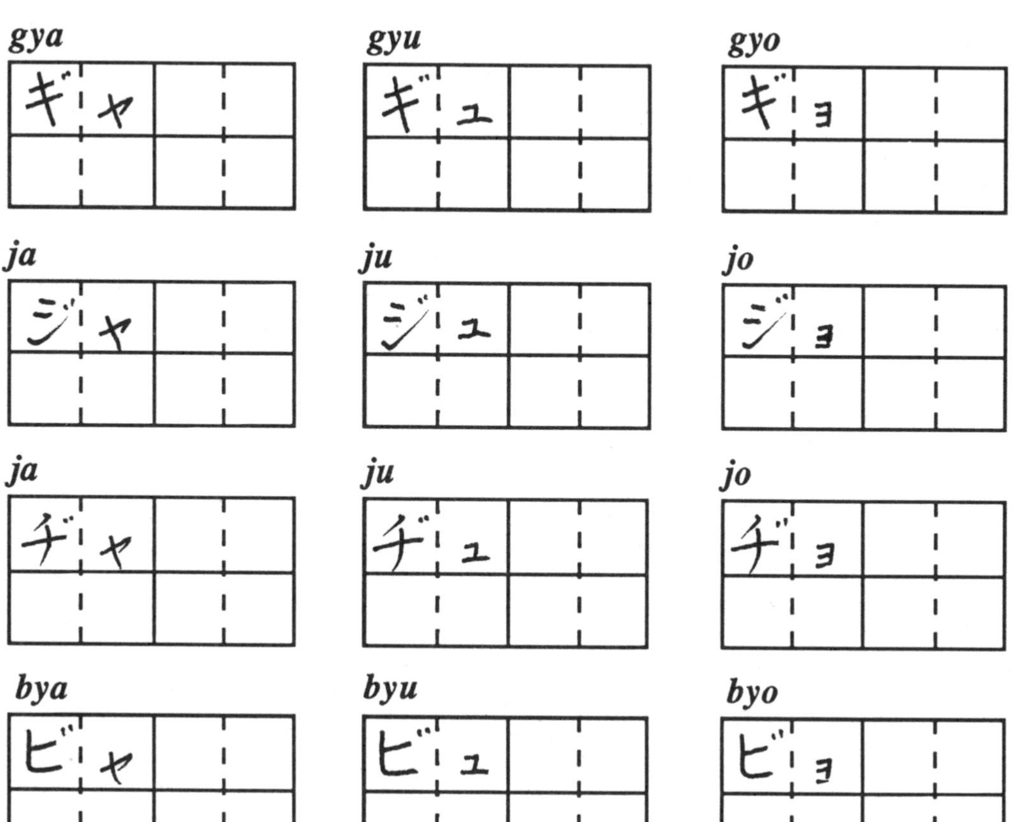

HALF-VOICED COMBINED SOUNDS *PYA—PYO* / ピャ—ピョ

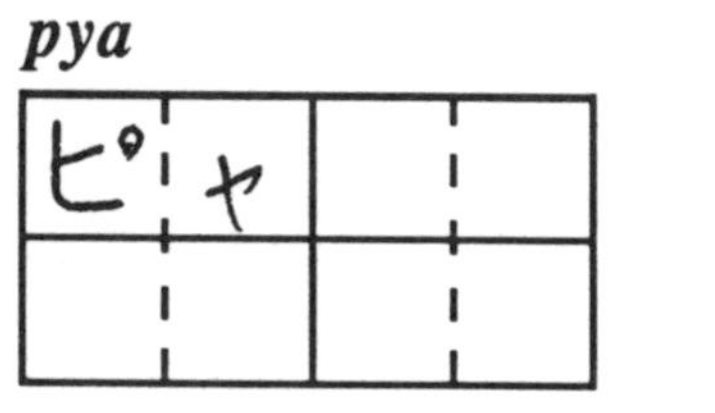

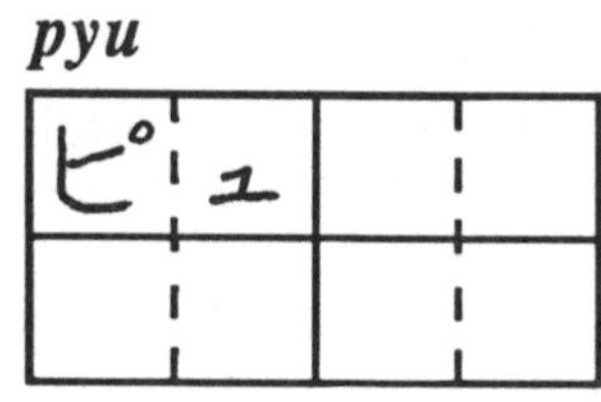

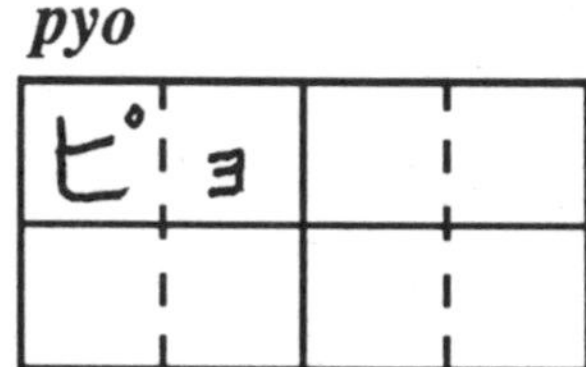

REVIEW OF COMBINED SOUNDS AND DOUBLE CONSONANTS

Katakana	Romaji	English
ショー	***shō***	show
ネット	***netto***	net
ファン	***fan***	fan (sports)
イェティ	***yeti***	yeti
ニュース	***nyūsu***	news
フォーク	***fōku***	fork; folk
チェック	***chekku***	check
ジェリー	***jerī***	jelly
チョーク	***chōku***	chalk
ウォッチ	***wotchi***	watch
ディスク	***disuku***	disk

fairu file

ファイル

wēbu/wēvu wave (hair)

ウェーヴ

bideo/video video

ヴィデオ

manshon apartment house

マンション

windō window

ウィンドー

mājan mahjong

マージャン

wētā waiter

ウェーター

kyasshu cash

キャッシュ

hyūman human

ヒューマン

pitchā pitcher (sports)

ピッチャー

duetto duet

デュエット

REVIEW THROUGH INTERNATIONAL PLACE NAMES

Ajia Asia

アジア

Suisu Switzerland

スイス

Rōma Rome

ローマ

Kanada Canada

カナダ

Doitsu Germany

ドイツ

Atene Athens

アテネ

Puraha Prague

プラハ

Amerika America

アメリカ

Oranda Holland

オランダ

Igirisu England

イギリス

Mekishiko Mexico

メキシコ

Mosukuwa Moscow

モスクワ

Betonamu Vietnam

ベトナム

Shidonī Sydney

シドニー

Kyūba Cuba

キューバ

Wīn Vienna

ウィーン

Furansu France

フランス

Yōroppa Europe

ヨーロッパ

Firipin Philippines

フィリピン

Bagudaddo Baghdad

バグダッド

Echiopia Ethiopia

エチオピア

Noruwē Norway

ノルウェー

Jakaruta Jakarta

ジャカルタ

Sanchiago Santiago

サンチアゴ

Pōtsumasu Portsmouth

ポーツマス

Hariuddo Hollywood

ハリウッド

Myunhen Munich

ミュンヘン

Guatemara Guatemala

グァテマラ

Maruseēyu Marseilles

マルセーユ

Betsurehemu Bethlehem

ベツレヘム

Dieppu Dieppe

ディエップ

Benechia/Venechia Venice

ヴェネチア

Chunijia/Tunijia Tunisia

テュニジア

III

FINAL REVIEW

ABOUT JAPAN

Copy each line in the space provided.

せかいちずをみましょう。にほ

んはアジアたいりくのひがしにあ

る、なんぼくにほそながいくにで

す。そのひろさはアメリカのカリ

フォルニアしゅうとだいたいおな

じです。よっつのおもなしまにわ

かれています。いちばんおおきい

のは、ほんしゅうで、このしまの

まんなかへんにとうきょうがあり

ます。ふじさんという、うつくし

いやまもあります。にばんめにお

おきいしまは、いちばんきたにあ
るほっかいどうで、なつはすずし
いですが、ふゆはさむくて、ゆき
がたくさんふりますから、スキー
やスケートができます。さんばん
めにおおきいきゅうしゅうは、み
なみにありますから、ふゆでもあ
たたかいです。よばんめのしこく
は、きたのほうはみかんで、みな
みのほうはさかなで、ゆうめいで
す。

FOOD ITEMS QUIZ

Fill in the blanks with appropriate romanization.

1. たまご ____________________ egg
2. パン ____________________ bread
3. コーヒー ____________________ coffee
4. かし ____________________ confectionery
5. ぶたにく ____________________ pork
6. ビール ____________________ beer
7. レモンティー ____________________ lemon tea
8. くだもの ____________________ fruit
9. しょうゆ ____________________ soy sauce
10. チーズ ____________________ cheese
11. バター ____________________ butter
12. オムレツ ____________________ omelette
13. やさい ____________________ vegetable
14. りんご ____________________ apple
15. ラーメン ____________________ Chinese noodles
16. ヨーグルト ____________________ yoghurt
17. さとう ____________________ sugar
18. ビスケット ____________________ biscuit
19. なっとう ____________________ fermented soybean
20. ジュース ____________________ juice
21. かずのこ ____________________ herring roe
22. プリン ____________________ custard pudding
23. みかん ____________________ mikan orange
24. パルフェ ____________________ parfait
25. ヴェニソン ____________________ venison

FLORA AND FAUNA QUIZ

Fill in the blanks with *hiragana* (H) or *katakana* (K) as appropriate.

1.	inu (H)	______________	dog
2.	sakana (H)	______________	fish
3.	raion (K)	______________	lion
4.	take (H)	______________	bamboo
5.	kaede (H)	______________	maple
6.	yūkari (K)	______________	eucalyptus
7.	tsubaki (H)	______________	camellia
8.	chūrippu (K)	______________	tulip
9.	maguro (H)	______________	tuna
10.	koara (K)	______________	koala bear
11.	nihonzaru (H)	______________	Japanese monkey
12.	kangarū (K)	______________	kangaroo
13.	nezumi (H)	______________	mouse, rat
14.	ajisai (H)	______________	hydrangea
15.	haibisukasu (K)	______________	hibiscus
16.	hyō (H)	______________	leopard
17.	kānēshon (K)	______________	carnation
18.	kabutomushi (H)	______________	Goliath beetle
19.	hebi (H)	______________	snake
20.	pengin (K)	______________	penguin
21.	hirame (H)	______________	flatfish
22.	botan (H)	______________	peony
23.	mahoganī (K)	______________	mahogany
24.	suisen (H)	______________	narcissus
25.	ichō (H)	______________	gingko

PERSONAL NAMES QUIZ

Underline the *kana* error in each name and write the correct version in the blank.

1.	じろお	____________	Jiro (Jirō)
2.	きャロル	____________	Carole (Kyaroru)
3.	ねいこ	____________	Reiko
4.	ノームン	____________	Norman (Nōman)
5.	とるお	____________	Teruo
6.	ウェソディー	____________	Wendy (Wendī)
7.	まサよし	____________	Masayoshi
8.	ヴァヌサ	____________	Vanessa (Vanesa)
9.	おけみ	____________	Akemi
10.	ドワート	____________	Dwight (Dowaito)
11.	けんいし	____________	Kenichi (Ken'ichi)
12.	シェーノ	____________	Shane (Shēn)
13.	ゆきい	____________	Yukiko
14.	ヂュリー	____________	Julie (Jurī)
15.	おりへ	____________	Orie
16.	ソウフィ	____________	Sophie (Sōfi)
17.	っとむ	____________	Tsutomu
18.	ウィリマム	____________	William (Wiriamu)
19.	ひでミ	____________	Hidemi
20.	ジャッタ	____________	Jack (Jakku)
21.	されこ	____________	Sawako
22.	デヴィっド	____________	David (Deviddo)
23.	のそむ	____________	Nozomu
24.	エリザペス	____________	Elizabeth (Erizabesu)
25.	ラッセル	____________	Russell (Rasseru)

KANA WORD SEARCH

ヌ	カ	い	ル	イ	サ	ミ	ま	エ	ラ	ヤ	う	く	れ	プ
ご	う	ウ	り	め	ね	キ	な	ジ	こ	つ	ぞ	め	ロ	ぬ
モ	ぜ	な	ン	あ	ま	ウ	オ	け	と	わ	り	ぺ	ぼ	ぶ
よ	ね	ほ	る	ト	わ	ホ	に	ス	ぎ	さ	ラ	ど	す	し
ら	そ	し	ぷ	ネ	し	せ	ス	ど	ク	と	る	む	う	パ
い	わ	つ	め	ズ	う	ち	ま	テ	レ	ビ	か	ふ	べ	ぐ
ア	お	れ	ユ	で	ま	も	ざ	た	ル	ア	ん	シ	さ	か
よ	ろ	い	に	し	ワ	る	ネ	あ	に	ゾ	じ	い	ね	す
や	る	ば	ん	が	ル	ト	だ	ナ	か	ん	げ	も	ゴ	ケ
ず	み	き	メ	グ	ツ	ン	イ	て	し	ら	ち	デ	ニ	ム
の	プ	せ	ふ	ぐ	ラ	ロ	ハ	え	は	た	パ	ヌ	び	ち
デ	そ	レ	ぽ	ゆ	ン	フ	が	タ	ポ	ソ	え	つ	ノ	む
ザ	て	お	ゼ	モ	き	ん	レ	る	コ	ひ	の	き	ろ	ま
イ	た	や	ゆ	ン	お	ン	け	ン	リ	ツ	ガ	み	ヒ	お
ン	く	へ	マ	ス	ト	ぬ	エ	ノ	み	つ	ヨ	こ	い	か

Find the fifty words below in the square above, moving in a straight line in any direction including diagonals. The first thirty words are in *hiragana,* the rest *katakana.* (We found over 200 other *hiragana* words, most of two symbols and not found elsewhere in this book. How many can you find? Fifty or more means you have a good vocabulary.)

* * * * *

madogiwazoku (staff passed over for promotion), *tsuridōgu* (fishing gear), *haragei* (nonverbal communication), *shitsurei* (rudeness), *kanji* (character), *fugu* (blowfish), *hinoki* (cypress), *kanemochi* (rich person), *ganbaru* (try your best), *daruma* (Buddha doll), *yuki* (snow), *tate* (verticality), *oya* (parent), *uchi* (home, inner group), *sewa* (care), *ongaeshi* (repayment of favor), *tsukimi* (moon viewing), *umeboshi* (pickled plum), *nemawashi* (behind-the-scenes maneuvering), *musubu* (bind), *nukeru* (be missing), *furusato* (hometown), *ame* (rain), *hosoi* (slender), *kaiko* (silkworm), *heta* (unskilled), *tanin* (stranger), *yoroi* (armor), *nama* (raw), *mizu* (water); *nairon, kiosuku, gurafu, dezain, terebi, hosuteru, warutsu, gasorin, furonto, puropera, purezento, kaunto, pasokon, misairu, tarento, rajio, gomu, masuto, denimu, yoga.* (Look up the *katakana* words you don't know.)

QUIZ ANSWERS

	Food items	Flora/fauna	Names
1.	tamago	いぬ	じろう
2.	pan	さかな	キャロル
3.	kōhī	ライオン	れいこ
4.	kashi	たけ	ノーマン
5.	butaniku	かえで	てるお
6.	bīru	ユーカリ	ウェンディー
7.	remon tī	つばき	まさよし
8.	kudamono	チューリップ	ヴァネサ
9.	shōyu	まぐろ	あけみ
10.	chīzu	コアラ	ドワイト
11.	batā	にほんざる	けんいち
12.	omuretsu	カンガルー	シェーン
13.	yasai	ねずみ	ゆきこ
14.	ringo	あじさい	ジュリー
15.	rāmen	ハイビスカス	おりえ
16.	yōguruto	ひょう	ソーフィ
17.	satō	カーネーション	つとむ
18.	bisuketto	かぶとむし	ウィリアム
19.	nattō	へび	ひでみ
20.	jūsu	ペンギン	ジャック
21.	kazunoko	ひらめ	さわこ
22.	purin	ぼたん	デヴィッド
23.	mikan	マホガニー	のぞむ
24.	parufe	すいせん	エリザベス
25.	benison/venison	いちょう	ラッセル

ENGLISH VERSION OF "ABOUT JAPAN"

Let's look at an atlas. Japan is a long, thin country lying on a north-south axis to the east of the Asian mainland. It's about the same size as the state of California in America. It consists of four main islands. The largest is Honshu, with Tokyo at its midpoint. The beautiful Mount Fuji is also found on this island. The next largest is Hokkaido, the northernmost island. Summer here is cool, and in winter heavy snow makes skiing and skating possible. Kyushu, the third largest island, lies to the south, so it's warm here even in winter. The fourth largest, Shikoku, is noted for mikan oranges from its northern half and fish from the south.

DO-IT-YOURSELF *KANA* CHARTS

Fill in the following charts, writing *hiragana* in the left part of each box and *katakana* in the right. Then check your entries against the charts in the Explanation of *Kana*.

Basic Kana Symbols

VOWELS

CONSONANTS	a	i	u	e	o
	a	i	u	e	o
k	ka	ki	ku	ke	ko
s	sa	shi	su	se	so
t	ta	chi	tsu	te	to
n	na	ni	nu	ne	no
h	ha	hi	fu	he	ho
m	ma	mi	mu	me	mo
y	ya		yu		yo
r	ra	ri	ru	re	ro
w	wa				wo
n	n				

Basic Voiced Sounds

	a	i	u	e	o
g	ga	gi	gu	ge	go
z/j	za	ji	zu	ze	zo
d/z/j	da	ji	zu	de	do
b	ba	bi	bu	be	bo
p	pa	pi	pu	pe	po

Basic Combinations

	a	u	o
ky	kya	kyu	kyo
sh	sha	shu	sho
ch	cha	chu	cho
ny	nya	nyu	nyo
hy	hya	hyu	hyo
my	mya	myu	myo
ry	rya	ryu	ryo

Voiced Combinations

	a	u	o
gy	gya	gyu	gyo
j	ja	ju	jo
j	ja	ju	jo
by	bya	byu	byo
py	pya	pyu	pyo

THE *IROHA* VERSE

The *iroha* verse was written about a thousand years ago. Though based upon a teaching of Buddhism its main use is for writing practice, for it includes all of the *kana* symbols with the exception of the final *n* (ん). In ancient times *mu* (む) was used where ん is used today. The order of symbols in the verse — particularly the first half dozen — is important because it is still sometimes followed in listings, in similar fashion to the English order "a, b, c."

Try copying out the verse in the space at the foot of the page.

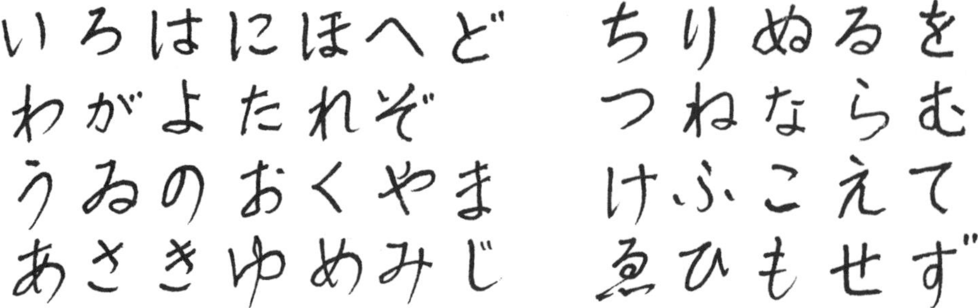

The modern romanized version is: *Iro wa nioedo chirinuru o / Waga yo tare zo tsune naran / Ui no okuyama kyō koete / Asaki yume miji ei mo sezu.*

A literal paraphrase is: "Colors are fragrant, but they fade away. In this world of ours none lasts forever. Today cross the high mountain of life's illusions [i.e., rise above this physical world], and there will be no more shallow dreaming, no more drunkenness [i.e., there will be no more uneasiness, no more temptations]."

The above translation is given in the appendices of the *Japanese - English Character Dictionary* (edited by A. Nelson, published by Charles E. Tuttle Company, 1962). Readers who wish to learn more about the historical use of *kana,* such as けふ for the modern きょう, are recommended to consult this work.